Cloud Computing - Applications and Sustainable Developments

Edited by Sultan Ahmad, Sudan Jha and Aasim Zafar

Published in London, United Kingdom

Cloud Computing - Applications and Sustainable Developments
http://dx.doi.org/10.5772/intechopen.1008010
Edited by Sultan Ahmad, Sudan Jha and Aasim Zafar

Contributors
Abdul Malik Maheen, Andrei Kazakin, Andrei Marchenko, C.S. Sree Thayanandeswari, Carlos Diego Cavalcanti Pereira, Deqian Fu, Dmitry Shchemelinin, Jinze Ma, Niyas Ahamed Sirajudeen, Qianhui Ma, Waleed Almuseelem, Yaxian Jing, Zanmei Wu, Zhanling Shi, Ziqi Liu

First published in London, United Kingdom, 2025 by IntechOpen
IntechOpen is the global imprint of INTECHOPEN LIMITED, registered in England and Wales, registration number: 11086078, 167-169 Great Portland Street, London, W1W 5PF, United Kingdom

For EU product safety concerns: IN TECH d.o.o., Prolaz Marije Krucifikse Kozulić 3, 51000 Rijeka, Croatia, info@intechopen.com or visit our website at intechopen.com.

British Library Cataloguing-in-Publication Data
A catalogue record for this book is available from the British Library

Cloud Computing - Applications and Sustainable Developments
Edited by Sultan Ahmad, Sudan Jha and Aasim Zafar
p. cm.
Print ISBN 978-1-83634-260-1
Online ISBN 978-1-83634-259-5
eBook (PDF) ISBN 978-1-83634-261-8

Meet the editors

Dr. Sultan Ahmad has been associated with the Department of Computer Science, College of Computer Engineering and Sciences, Prince Sattam Bin Abdulaziz University, Alkharj, Saudi Arabia. He is also an Adjunct Professor with Chandigarh University, Gharuan, Punjab, India. He received his Master of Computer Science and Applications from Aligarh Muslim University, India, in 2006, and his Ph.D. degree in CSE from Glocal University. He has more than 18 years of teaching and research experience. He has around 150 accepted and published research papers and book chapters in reputed SCI, SCIE, ESCI, and SCOPUS-indexed journals and conferences. He also serves as a Guest Editor for SCIE/ESCI/SCOPUS-indexed journals. He holds Australian, Chinese, Indian, and two UK design patents in his name. He has authored and edited 10 books on cutting-edge topics. His research has also secured funding from national and international projects. He also took up the roles of resource person and technical panel member and headed several international conferences. He has presented his research papers at many national and international conferences. He has been involved in many research projects as a principal and co-principal investigator. He has been an integral part of the university's accreditation processes, including ABET and NCAAA. His research interests include Intelligent computing, data Science, machine learning, and Internet of Things. He is a member of IEEE, IACSIT, and the Computer Society of India.

Dr. Sudan Jha is a Senior member of IEEE and a Professor in the Department of Computer Science & Engineering at Kathmandu University, Nepal, with over 23 years of combined teaching, research, and industrial experience. He is a lead researcher of the IoT R&D lab at Kathmandu University. His previous affiliations include KIIT University, Chandigarh University, Christ University, etc. He was 'Technical Director' at Nepal Television, 'Principal' at Nepal College of IT, and 'Individual Consultant' at Nepal Telecom Authority. He is dedicated to advancing higher education quality and actively works on smart platforms. His extensive research portfolio comprises 85+ SCI, SCIE-indexed research papers and book chapters in international peer-reviewed journals and conferences. He serves as a Co-Editor-in-Chief in an international journal. He also serves as a Guest Editor for SCIE/ESCI/SCOPUS-indexed journals. With three patents to his name, he has authored and edited 7 books on cutting-edge topics in IoT, 5G, and AI, published by Elsevier, CRC, and AAP. His research has also secured funding for two international projects. Additionally, he serves as a keynote speaker at over 40 international conferences. In addition, he has delivered faculty development programs, short-term training programs, and workshops at national and international conferences, as well as universities. He holds certifications in Microservices Architecture, Data Science, and Foundations of Artificial Intelligence. His primary research interests encompass Quality of Services in IoT-enabled devices, Neutrosophic theory, and Neutrosophic Soft Set Systems.

Dr. Aasim Zafar is a Professor in the Computer Science Department at Aligarh Muslim University, Aligarh, India. He holds a Master's degree in Computer Science and Applications and obtained a Ph.D. in Computer Science from Aligarh Muslim University, Aligarh, India. His research areas and special interests include Mobile Ad hoc and Sensor Networks, Image Processing and Video Analytics, Information Retrieval, E-Systems, e-Security, Virtual Learning Environment, Neuro-Fuzzy and Soft Computing, and Software Engineering. His areas of teaching interest include Computer Networks, Network Security, Software Engineering, E-Systems, Database Management Systems and Computer Programming. He has presented numerous papers at national and international conferences and published various research papers in reputable international journals. He has over 32 years of teaching and research experience, spanning both national and international levels. He has executed the NMEICT-EdRP project funded by MHRD, Govt. of India as Co-PI, which was executed in consortium mode with AMU being one of the partner institutions (with a share of Rs 1. 2 crore) and IIT, Kanpur being the Coordinating Institute. AMU successfully contributed two major outcomes, namely, a cloud-based multi-lingual and multi-institutional Library Management System (LibMS) and Election Management System (EMS) to this project. During his 5-year tenure of an International teaching assignment at King Abdulaziz University (KAU), Jeddah, he has executed three research projects, two DSR-funded (SR 50,000 each) as PI and one funded by KACST (SR 2 Million) as Co-PI. He was awarded the "Excellence in Teaching Award" at KAU, Jeddah. Besides teaching and research, he has a rich administrative experience and is actively involved in various developmental work of the university in various capacities. Presently, he has been assigned additional responsibility in administration as Officer-on-Special Duty (Development), AMU since 11. 05. 2024. He has served as Chairperson/Head of the Department of Computer Science from January 19, 2021, to January 18, 2024. He is currently the UGC SWAYAM Coordinator, Coordinator of the IGNOU Study Centre at AMU, Convener of the University Website Committee, Convener of the Digital Monitoring Cell, Member of the CIQA, CDOE, AMU, and a member of various high-powered committees constituted by the Hon'ble Vice Chancellor of AMU. He has made immense contributions to the University's ICT Infrastructure Development. At KAU, Prof. Zafar successfully led the Academic Accreditation Unit of FCIT, KAU, in the capacity of Director to achieve ABET (American Accreditation Board of Engineering and Technology) accreditation. As SWAYAM Coordinator, he has taken the initiative and successfully led the development and launch of 31 MOOCs for the July 2024 semester and 22 MOOCs for the January 2025 semester on the SWAYAM Platform by the faculty members of AMU (INI). Prof. Aasim Zafar has been actively working in the area of e-learning and utilizing Open-Source ICT Tools and Technologies in Research, teaching, and learning, as well as student evaluation, since 1995, both at the Graduate and Postgraduate levels. He has served CDOE and AMU as Coordinator of e-Learning Programmes. He has expertise in Educational Technologies and contributed to spreading the culture of ICT-enabled Pedagogy among teachers of HEIs through various workshops, orientations, trainings, and capacity-building programmes. He has also organized various webinars, workshops, and training programs on e-content development and ICT-related topics. Prof. Aasim Zafar is a valuable resource person and delivered skill based technical sessions/lectures across the country for Faculty Development Programmes [FDP], Faculty Induction Programmes [FIP], Refresher Courses and Orientation Programmes at UGC HRDCs and different Universities in India on e-Learning, SWAYAM MOOCs, e-Content Development, Capacity building for blended learning, Educational Technologies for Online Teaching and Learning, Learning Management Systems (LMS), and e-Governance, etc. He has trained over 5000 faculty members from various universities/colleges across the country in online teaching and learning since March 2020, during the COVID-19 pandemic.

Contents

Preface IX

Chapter 1 1
Sustainable Developments in Cloud Computing and Its Applications
by Niyas Ahamed Sirajudeen, C.S. Sree Thayanandeswari and Abdul Malik Maheen

Chapter 2 25
Capacity Planning of Cloud Computing Workloads
by Carlos Diego Cavalcanti Pereira

Chapter 3 45
Perspective Chapter: Trusted and Intelligent Cloud Computing for Logistics Industry Alliance
by Deqian Fu, Yaxian Jing, Ziqi Liu, Zhanling Shi, Zanmei Wu, Jinze Ma and Qianhui Ma

Chapter 4 59
Orchestrating Data Center Bring-Up: Efficient Strategies for Scalable Infrastructure Deployment
by Dmitry Shchemelinin, Andrei Kazakin and Andrei Marchenko

Chapter 5 79
Exploring the Impact of AI-Driven Cybersecurity Frameworks on Data Privacy, Security, and Resource Optimization in Cloud Environments
by Waleed Almuseelem

Preface

Cloud computing has emerged as a foundational technology driving innovation across virtually every sector of modern society. Its ability to deliver scalable, on-demand computing resources transcends traditional IT boundaries, enabling unprecedented solutions to complex global challenges. *Cloud Computing – Applications and Sustainable Developments* explores this transformative potential, focusing specifically on how cloud technologies are being harnessed to foster environmental stewardship, enhance social equity, and build resilient, efficient systems for a sustainable future.

This volume brings together cutting-edge research and practical insights from leading experts worldwide. The selected chapters delve into diverse applications, demonstrating how cloud computing serves as a critical enabler for sustainable development. From optimizing logistics networks and revolutionizing energy management through artificial intelligence, to modernizing government services and educational data systems, the cloud provides the agility and computational power necessary for impactful solutions.

Readers will discover strategies for orchestrating scalable, energy-efficient data center infrastructure – a cornerstone of sustainable cloud operations. They will explore the conceptual and practical foundations of cloud databases, the implementation of cloud-based academic systems promoting accessibility, and sophisticated methods for cloud workload capacity planning. The book further examines the integration of AI with cloud platforms to enhance power grid stability and efficiency, and showcases how "GovTech" leverages the cloud to deliver smarter, more responsive public services.

Published by IntechOpen, this book reflects our commitment to disseminating high-quality, peer-reviewed knowledge openly and globally. We aim to provide researchers, practitioners, policymakers, and students with a comprehensive resource that illuminates the vital intersection of cloud computing and sustainability. The insights contained within these pages offer valuable perspectives for driving technological advancement in harmony with the needs of our planet and its people.

Sultan Ahmad
Department of Computer Science,
College of Computer Engineering and Sciences,
Prince Sattam Bin Abdulaziz University,
Alkharj, Saudi Arabia

Sudan Jha
Department of Computer Science and Engineering,
Kathmandu University,
Dhulikhel, Nepal

Aasim Zafar
Computer Science Department,
Aligarh Muslim University,
Aligarh, India

Chapter 1

Sustainable Developments in Cloud Computing and Its Applications

Niyas Ahamed Sirajudeen, C.S. Sree Thayanandeswari and Abdul Malik Maheen

Abstract

Cloud computing's rapid growth has transformed digital infrastructure by making it scalable, flexible, and more cost-effective. Still, the increasing use of energy and the resulting environmental problems make it difficult for the industry to be sustainable. In this chapter, we examine how green technologies and energy-saving architectures are used in sustainable cloud computing. Solutions discussed include running data centers with renewable energy, using virtual servers to improve resource usage, and applying AI to manage energy use. In addition, the chapter discusses techniques for managing workloads such as energy-aware planning, smart placement of workloads, and neutral carbon operations. Case studies and empirical analysis are used to show how major cloud service providers and enterprises have successfully implemented cloud computing. The research points out that putting sustainability into practice helps the environment and also benefits businesses over the long run. This chapter helps researchers, developers, industry experts, and policymakers find ways to balance new technology with care for the environment.

Keywords: sustainable cloud computing, green technologies, energy efficiency, server virtualization, renewable energy, workload optimization, carbon-neutral operations

1. Introduction

The digital era relies heavily on cloud computing that has greatly changed how data is handled in different industries. It makes it possible to use servers, storage, and applications whenever needed through the internet, so there is no need for local hardware [1]. As a result, digital services have seen a lot of new developments, allowing businesses, governments, and individuals to expand quickly, become more efficient, and cut down on initial investment costs. For this reason, cloud computing is now a key driver of the Fourth Industrial Revolution. The quick growth of cloud services around the world has encouraged hyperscale providers such as Amazon Web Services (AWS), Microsoft Azure, and Google Cloud to build huge data centers. They are built in different continents to ensure high availability, quicker connections, and stronger resilience [2]. Market research shows that the cloud computing market reached over $600 billion in 2023 and is still expanding at a fast double-digit CAGR. The main reasons for this fast growth are the growing use of digital services and the important role cloud technology has in helping businesses, schools, hospitals, and government offices become digital. Even so, as technology advances, we are also facing a new environmental problem. Since cloud infrastructure is used everywhere, it leads to a lot of energy use because servers, cooling systems, and power supply units are always running in data centers [3]. It is estimated that worldwide, data centers use approximately 1–2% of the planet's electricity and this number is expected to rise as data, AI, and streaming services become more common. Traditional energy sources used by data centers also add to the urgent problem of global climate change. Because of these implications, more and more policymakers, researchers, and industry leaders are concerned.

Cloud computing is praised for saving money and being responsive, but now, its environmental impact is being examined more closely. Because of the rising importance of ESG, stakeholders are now considering the future effects of inefficient cloud systems [4]. It covers checking the emissions from data center building, running the centers, and recycling hardware and the indirect environmental results of nonstop services. As a result, more attention is being given to making cloud computing models that are both environmentally friendly and technologically advanced. This means using renewable energy in data centers, designing energy-saving hardware, optimizing how work is done, and using AI to control energy use. This chapter will discuss how sustainable cloud computing is not only a possible technology but a vital strategy to avoid damaging the environment as digital growth increases [1]. Although there has been progress, there are still many limits to today's sustainable cloud computing models. Many data centers still use nonrenewable energy because the local grid is not equipped for solar or wind integration. Although existing virtualization and workload optimization tools are successful in cutting down on idle servers, they are not always able to handle sudden changes in data loads that results in poor resource usage. In addition, AI-based energy management systems need a lot of data and powerful computers that actually leads to more energy being used.

Due to a lack of standardization, green cloud frameworks are not implemented the same way by every provider. It is also difficult to compare companies because there are many different ways to measure sustainability and track carbon. As these models have formed the basis for green cloud architecture, carbon-aware load balancing, and energy-aware VM placement, they still need to be improved, linked to policy frameworks, and adopted more widely to reduce environmental impact fully.

1.1 Key contribution

Following is the key contribution of the study,

- Green infrastructure implementation: Demonstrates the integration of renewable energy sources (e.g., solar, wind) and virtual server technologies to reduce the carbon footprint and enhance energy efficiency in cloud environments.

- AI-driven energy management: Introduces artificial intelligence-based approaches for optimizing energy consumption through intelligent monitoring, dynamic workload scheduling, and predictive resource allocation.

- Workload optimization for sustainability: Explores techniques such as energy-aware workload planning, smart task placement, and load balancing to minimize energy waste and improve overall system efficiency.

- Evidence-based industry practices: Presents real-world case studies and empirical analysis from major cloud service providers to validate the effectiveness and impact of sustainable cloud strategies.

- Strategic guidance for stakeholders: Provides actionable insights and a road map for researchers, developers, industry leaders, and policymakers to promote and adopt sustainable practices in the evolving cloud computing landscape.

2. Green cloud technologies and sustainable architecture

Because cloud computing is growing so fast, people are now worried about its impact on energy and the environment. Green cloud technologies are designed to lower the amount of carbon produced by cloud services by adopting sustainable methods and making changes to architecture [3]. The main aim is to make the best use of resources and reduce both energy use and harm to the environment. Because of virtualization, several virtual machines (VMs) can be run on one physical server that increases hardware efficiency and decreases the number of physical servers needed. As a result of consolidation, data centers use less electricity, need less cooling, and take up less space [5]. Containers are a simpler option than VMs since they use the host OS kernel and separate each application they run. As a result, the company uses fewer resources, deploys systems more quickly, and saves energy. These systems watch the energy usage of data center equipment and assign tasks depending on how efficiently they can be run. They use workload merging, DVFS, and turning off unused servers to conserve energy. Thus, **Table 1** shows the comparison between traditional cloud architecture and green cloud architecture.

Feature	Traditional cloud architecture	Green cloud architecture
Server utilization	Low to moderate; many idle servers	High utilization through virtualization and containers
Resource management	Static allocation of resources	Dynamic, energy-aware resource management
Energy consumption	High; no optimization for power efficiency	Optimized using energy-aware algorithms
Cooling requirements	Constant, often excessive cooling	Reduced through improved server utilization and cooling techniques
Hardware deployment	Large number of physical servers	Fewer physical servers due to consolidation
Deployment speed	Slower due to VM overhead and static provisioning	Faster *via* containerization and automated scaling
Operational costs	Higher energy and maintenance costs	Lower due to energy efficiency and resource optimization
Environmental impact	Significant carbon footprint	Reduced carbon footprint through sustainable practices
Monitoring and control	Basic monitoring with limited energy control	Advanced monitoring integrating energy consumption data
Scalability	Manual or semiautomated scaling	Automated, energy-efficient scaling

Table 1.
Comparison between traditional cloud architecture and green cloud architecture [1–6].

Since cloud computing is expanding so rapidly, many now concern about its effects on energy and the environment. By using green cloud technologies, less carbon is produced outstanding to the use of sustainable methods and changes in architecture. The main objective is to make the most out of resources and lessen both energy use and harm to the environment [4]. Thanks to virtualization, one physical server can run several virtual machines that makes hardware more efficient and saves on the number of servers needed. Because of consolidation, data centers use less energy, require less cooling, and occupy less space. Containers are an easier choice than VMs because they share the host OS kernel and keep each application in its own space. As a consequence, the company needs less energy, can deploy systems faster, and uses fewer resources. These systems observe the power consumption of data center equipment and allocate jobs based on their efficiency. They merge their workloads, use DVFS, and turn off extra servers to reduce energy usage [1]. To support sustainability even more, green cloud systems now include live energy monitoring and management. They are designed to always watch the power usage of the CPU, GPU, memory, and network devices. Using the data, cloud management platforms can change how tasks are distributed and resources are used to focus on running them on the most energy-efficient hardware or at times when the grid's carbon intensity is low. Thanks to this approach, data centers can use less energy and reach their most efficient power levels which cuts down on waste (**Figure 1**).

Another important approach to green cloud sustainability is to add renewable energy sources. Solar, wind, or hydroelectric energy is being used more often in data centers, sometimes directly and sometimes through renewable energy credits. This change lowers our use of fossil fuels and greatly decreases greenhouse gas emissions [3]. Certain cloud providers are investigating placing data centers in various regions to benefit from the availability of renewable energy and to move workloads depending on the supply and demand of renewable energy. By choosing smart energy, cloud operations are in line with both environmental targets and regulations. In the future, green cloud architecture will use new ways to cool systems and rely more on AI for

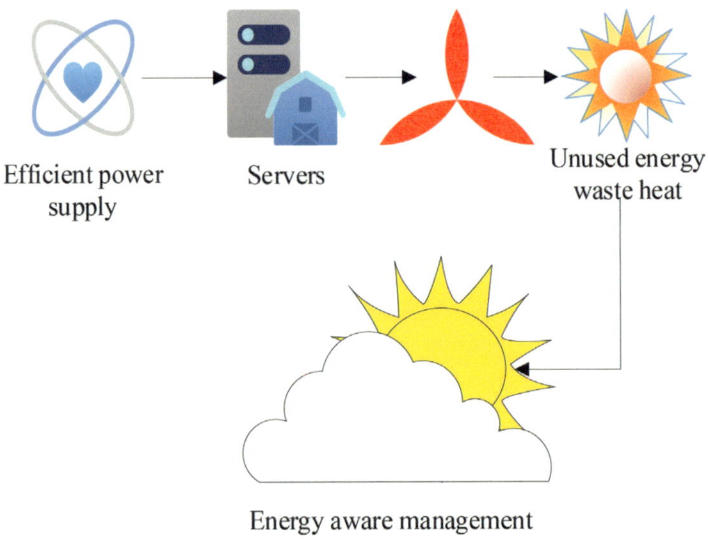

Figure 1.
Energy flow in green data centers.

automation. With liquid cooling, immersion cooling, and using waste heat for district heating, data center cooling causes less harm to the environment, as it historically has used a lot of energy [4]. AI can also be used by management systems to predict the amount of work needed and the environment, helping to optimize server use and cooling instantly. With these technologies, cloud infrastructure will become much more sustainable, helping to create a greener digital world [7]. Green data centers start with systems that provide power efficiently to reduce energy wastage. With virtualization and containerization, energy is allocated to servers in a way that helps them use more power for each watt consumed. Such systems use intelligent methods to share tasks, cut down on idle time, and switch off unused servers. Cooling systems make use of free cooling and liquid cooling which helps them use less power. The goal is to use less energy and produce more output, with less waste heat and emissions.

3. Renewable energy-powered data centers

Because more people use cloud computing and digital services, energy use in data centers has grown rapidly worldwide. Most data centers use grid electricity that is often made from fossil fuels and leads to a lot of greenhouse gas emissions. To reduce their environmental footprint, many firms are switching to data centers that are powered by solar, wind, and hydroelectric energy. This change helps the world reduce its carbon emissions and create greener IT systems. Renewable energy-based data centers have a much smaller impact on the environment than traditional centers [8]. Using clean energy, these facilities help to lower CO_2 emissions and air pollution. Also, renewable energy helps keep costs steady over the long run because it is not as affected by changes in fuel prices. By using this approach, companies can achieve their social responsibility targets and meet the tougher rules set by the environment. Solar energy is one of the most popular renewable options used in data centers. Electricity for data centers can be generated either by solar panels on the site or at nearby solar farms. Solar energy is now affordable because of progress in photovoltaic technology and lower costs. Some data centers use solar energy and batteries to keep working, even when there is no sunlight. Wind power is an important renewable energy that is used to operate data centers. Data centers are supplied with clean electricity from wind farms in areas where the wind is strong, either by direct connection or by purchase. Wind energy is handled by linking it to the grid and using other energy sources that can fill in the gaps. Using wind energy, companies add variety to their renewable sources and become stronger against interruptions in energy supply. Rivers and reservoirs are used by hydroelectric power plants to supply data centers with renewable energy that is reliable and steady. The fact that hydropower generates a lot of electricity without producing much pollution makes it worthwhile [1]. A lot of renewable energy agreements include hydroelectricity to help balance the unpredictable output from solar and wind. A number of technology leaders are leading the way in using renewable energy for their data centers. Google uses only renewable energy for its entire global operations and continues to back new renewable initiatives (**Figure 2**).

By 2030, Microsoft plans to become carbon negative, using renewable energy in all its data centers and taking out more carbon than it puts out. AWS has set a goal to use only renewable energy for its infrastructure by 2025 and is currently one of the biggest corporate purchasers of renewable energy globally. A lot of companies have set challenging goals for carbon neutrality and net-zero emissions to lead their

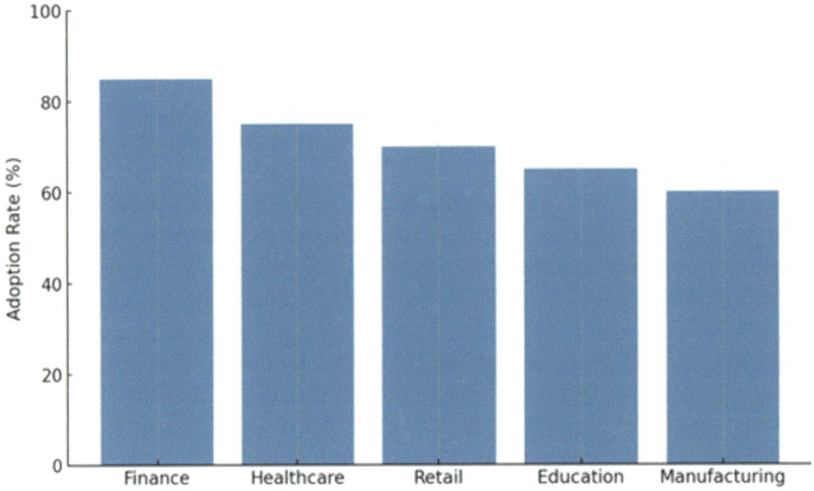

Figure 2.
Graphical representation of cloud adoption by industry.

renewable energy changes. These targets involve buying renewable energy certificates (RECs), investing in creating energy on site, and making energy use more efficient [5]. Often, reaching these goals depends on using comprehensive sustainability plans that handle energy, waste reduction, and supply chain management. Even though adopting renewable energy is very beneficial, it still faces problems such as unpredictable power supply, location barriers, and issues with the grid. Firms deal with these challenges by using various renewables, energy storage, and participating in regional power markets. Smart grid technology and demand response programs improve how the power system is integrated and made reliable (**Table 2**).

In the future, using green hydrogen, DC microgrids and AI to control energy in data centers is expected to improve the use of renewable energy. Teamwork among governments, industry, and utilities will be necessary to grow the use of renewable energy. Sharing more information about using renewable energy will help ensure we move forward and stay accountable. Using renewable energy in data centers is very important for decreasing the environmental effects of the digital economy. By investing wisely and advancing technology, companies can achieve zero carbon emissions, boost their efficiency, and help achieve global sustainability goals. Moving toward renewable energy will strengthen the IT infrastructure for years to come.

Metric	Traditional data centers	Renewable energy-powered data centers
Average power consumption (MW)	10	10
% Energy from renewable sources	<5%	60–100%
CO_2 emissions (tons/year)	20,000	2000–0
Renewable energy investment ($B)	0.1	2.5
% Reduction in energy costs	0%	10–20%
Carbon neutrality target year	N/A	2025–2030

Table 2.
Energy consumption, emissions, and investment metrics in traditional vs. renewable energy-powered data centers [7, 8].

4. AI and smart energy management in cloud operations

With cloud computing growing, the use of energy in data centers is now a major issue for both financial reasons and the environment. Manually managing energy is not enough to handle the changing and challenging workloads found in today's cloud environments. AI managing energy more efficiently and saving a lot of energy is now possible [9]. AI algorithms analysis a lot of operational data, including how workloads are distributed, how servers are used, and environmental conditions, to decide how resources should be allocated. AI helps allocate resources so that computing power is available when and where it is needed, preventing both overuse and lack of use that are big contributors to energy waste. AI is used widely for scheduling workloads as they change. AI systems review the current condition of the data center and assign tasks to servers that are both efficient and use the least amount of energy. With this system, loads are managed so fewer servers are needed, allowing idle machines to use less energy [10]. AI predictive maintenance allows us to find out which hardware is about to fail or use too much energy, so we can replace or repair them ahead of time. It helps to prevent wasted energy from inefficient hardware that reduces downtime and makes cloud operations more efficient. A big part of a data center's energy costs goes to cooling their systems. AI systems are always checking temperature, humidity, and airflow to adjust the cooling system in real time. With the help of AI, cooling systems can use less energy and still keep the environment safe (**Figure 3**).

AI helps make it easier to use renewable energy in cloud computing. AI can help manage when energy-intensive tasks are done by predicting when solar or wind power will be at its highest. As a result, less energy comes from nonrenewable sources and more comes from clean sources. AI is used by smart energy management systems to analyze and report on how energy is being used. Thanks to these insights, cloud operators can see what needs to be improved, compare their performance, and monitor their progress toward being more sustainable. AI-assisted reporting helps make decisions based on data and keeps businesses improving. AI makes it possible for virtualization and container orchestration to run more efficiently by organizing workloads, so fewer servers are used without affecting performance [8]. By doing this,

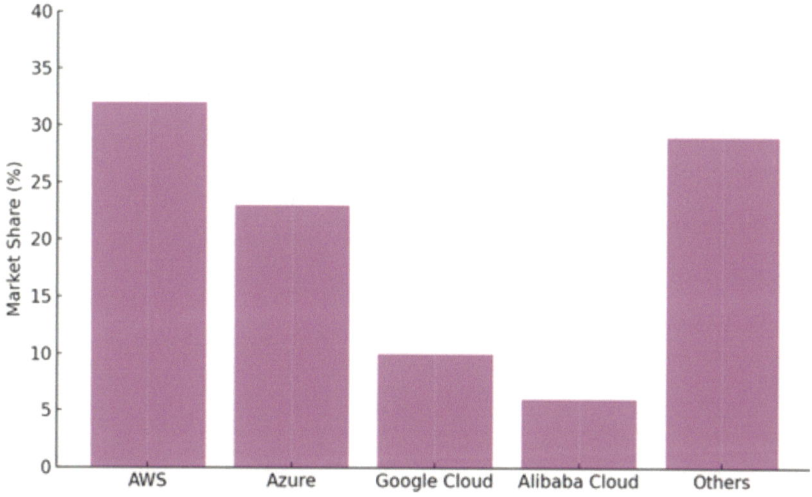

Figure 3.
IaaS cloud providers market share (%).

fewer physical servers are needed that leads to a decrease in energy use and advances green cloud objectives. Although AI is very helpful, it is important to deal with issues such as privacy, bias in algorithms, and how decisions are made. We should also pay attention to the energy used by AI models to ensure we are saving more energy than we use. For smart energy management to be sustainable, responsible AI design and use are necessary. AI in smart energy management will move toward cloud operations that let AI systems adjust and learn automatically as situations and demands change. Improvements in edge AI, federated learning, and AI hardware accelerators will make things more efficient. AI will play a key role in making cloud infrastructures perform well and be environmentally friendly. Key AI techniques for smart energy management in cloud operations are discussed as follows,

4.1 Load balancing that changes over time

Dynamic load balancing is a method that uses AI to move computing tasks from one server to another in real time, helping to save energy and make better use of resources. AI algorithms are always checking the performance of servers, how much power they use, and how much work is being done. Using dynamic load balancing, workload changes are predicted and tasks are moved to the servers that use the least energy that helps prevent overloading and cuts down on servers that are not working at full capacity [11]. As a result, fewer resources are left on and some servers can either use less energy or be turned off for a while. As a result, data centers use energy more efficiently and operate better (**Figure 4**).

4.2 Predictive cooling

Energy used for cooling in data centers can be as much as 40% of the total, so it is important to optimize these systems. Predictive cooling relies on AI to analyze previous and ongoing environmental data such as temperature, humidity, and airflow, to figure out how much cooling is needed. Predictive cooling units are different from others because they change the amount of cooling and airflow based on expected heat loads. It prevents the hardware from getting too cold and helps you use less energy [2].

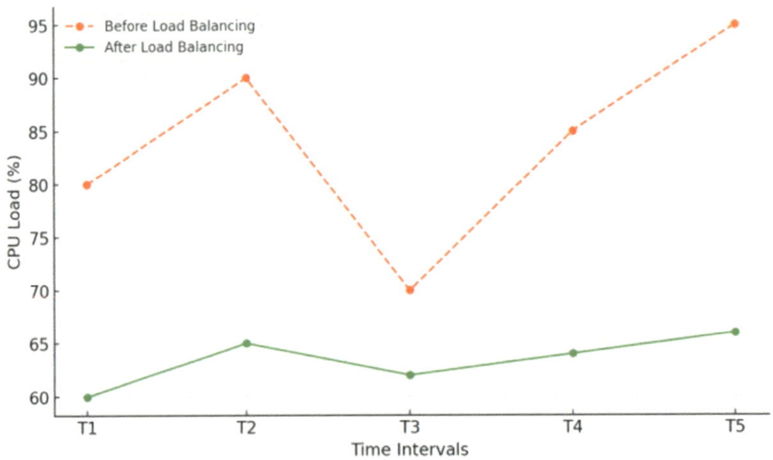

Figure 4.
Server load distribution over time.

DOI: http://dx.doi.org/10.5772/intechopen.1011479

Using AI and IoT sensors around the facility gives more detailed data to help improve predictions and make local changes to the cooling system (**Figure 5**).

4.3 Auto-scaling depending on real-time demand

Auto-scaling involves automatically increasing or decreasing computing resources like CPU, memory, and storage based on current demand. AI-based auto-scaling systems monitor the amount of work coming in, estimate upcoming changes in demand, and automatically add or remove virtual machines or containers as needed. It avoids problems from over-provisioning, where unused energy is wasted and under-provisioning that can lead to poor performance [12]. Auto-scaling matches the number of resources to the amount needed, so energy use is reduced without affecting service quality. AI algorithms can also factor in the availability of renewable energy to scale up operations when there is more green energy (**Figure 6**).

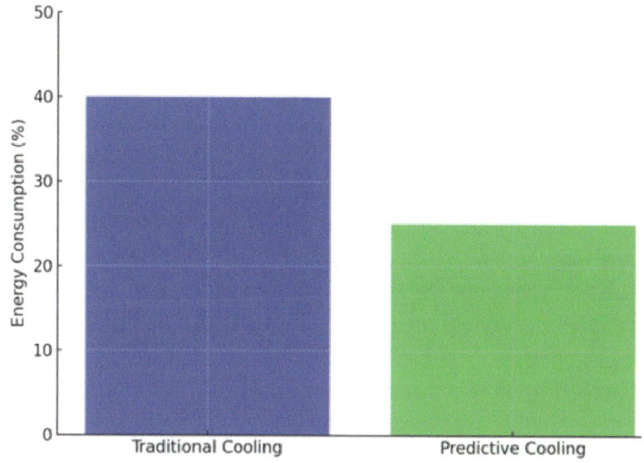

Figure 5.
Comparison of cooling energy comparison.

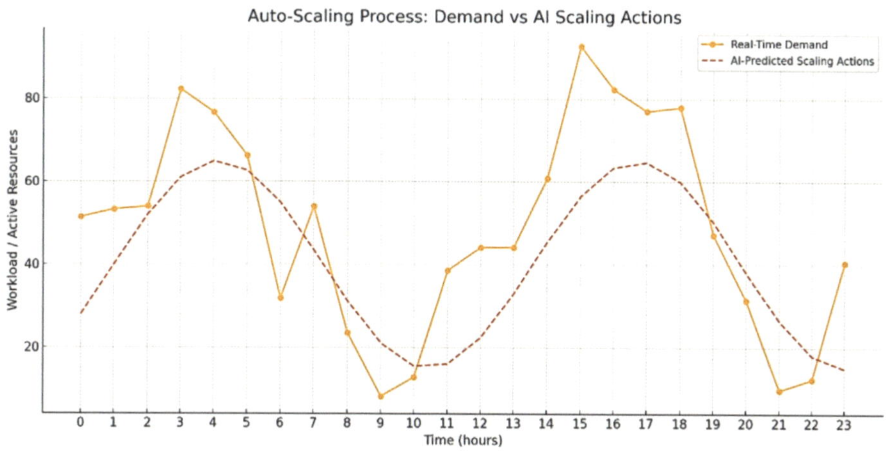

Figure 6.
Auto scaling process: demand vs. AI scaling actions.

5. Sustainable workload optimization and virtualization

Sustainable workload optimization is the intentional distribution and scheduling of computational workloads within cloud or virtualized environments with the goal of reducing energy usage while preserving performance. Energy efficiency is critical in today's data centers because servers tend to operate at reduced capacities, using power even when partly idle [9]. Virtualization is vital in that it makes it possible to run multiple workloads on fewer hardware machines using virtual machines (VMs) or containers. Effective workload optimization ensures that workloads are allocated to resources dynamically, preventing over-provisioning and minimizing the carbon emissions of IT infrastructure. Workload scheduling has a direct impact on the energy dynamics of virtualized environments [7]. Classic static scheduling methods seldom respond to real-time variations in resource demands, resulting in idle resources or wasted energy. Energy-aware scheduling algorithms, on the other hand, analyze the energy profiles of VMs and physical servers, placing workloads onto fewer active machines and shutting down idle nodes. Technologies such as dynamic voltage and frequency scaling (DVFS), thermal-aware scheduling, and green load balancing are combined with virtualization to provide the best energy utilization without compromising service-level agreements (SLAs) (**Table 3**).

Virtualization software like VMware, KVM, and Xen hypervisors, and container orchestration software like Kubernetes and Docker enable dynamic resource allocation and workload isolation. These platforms facilitate live VM or container migration such that workloads can migrate seamlessly according to energy-aware scheduling policies. By maximizing server utilization levels and facilitating dynamic consolidation, virtualization reduces over-provisioning needs. This results in decreased cooling needs, less utilization of physical hardware, and ultimately adds up to a greener computing setup (**Figure 7**).

Optimized scheduling of workload, when combined with smart virtualization platforms, delivers several sustainability advantages: lower operating expenses, greater energy efficiency, and lesser carbon footprint. Some emerging technologies like AI-based scheduling, predictive analytics, and edge virtualization are setting the stage for much smarter and greener workload management [9]. The addition of renewable sources of energy to data centers additionally boosts environmental advantages.

5.1 Server consolidation

Server consolidation is a data center strategy that aims to decrease the number of physical servers by consolidating several workloads onto fewer physical machines through virtualization [11]. It is at the core of sustainable computer practices since it

Scheduling technique	Adaptability	Energy efficiency	Resource utilization	Scalability
Static scheduling	Low	Poor	Low	Moderate
Round-robin scheduling	Moderate	Fair	Moderate	High
Energy-aware scheduling	High	Excellent	High	High
Thermal-aware load balancing	High	Very good	High	High

Table 3.
Comparison of workload scheduling techniques [5, 7, 8].

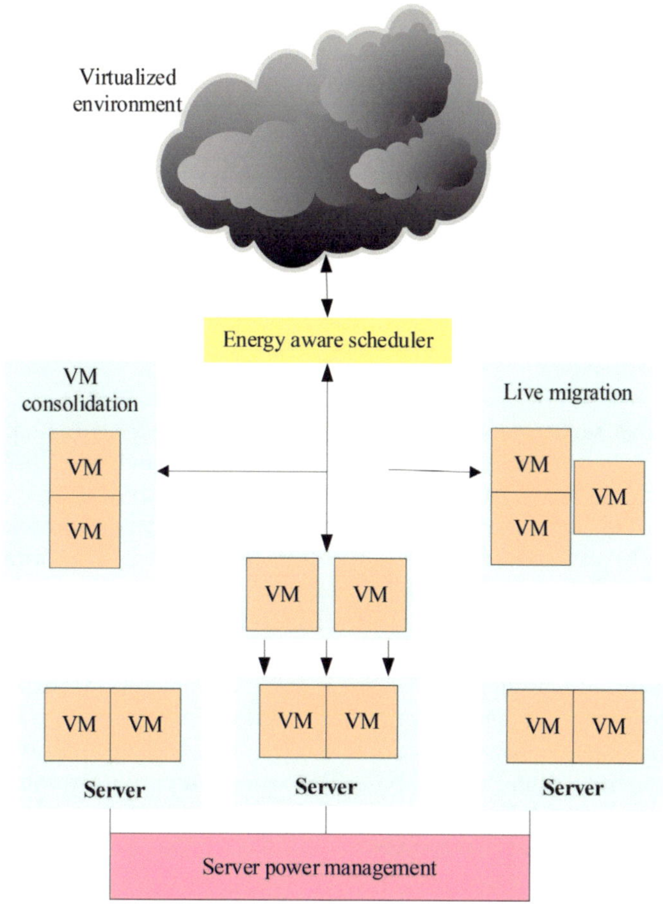

Figure 7.
Conceptual model for sustainable workload optimization in virtualized environment.

results in more efficient use of resources, reduces power utilization, and minimizes cooling. In virtualized environments, server consolidation supports many virtual machines (VMs) running at the same time on one physical server, hence cutting down on hardware redundancy and idle energy consumption. The process of consolidation is usually initiated by workload analysis, determining underutilized servers and workloads that can be co-located [10]. Hypervisors or container-based virtualization (for example, VMware ESXi, Hyper-V, KVM, Docker) are used to move such workloads into fewer physical hosts. Software such as live migration facilitates dynamic transfer of VMs without disruption, allowing transparent consolidation with continued services. Monitoring tools, supporting such a strategy, evaluate CPU, memory, disk, and network usage to determine the best consolidation opportunities. Server consolidation is a key to saving energy. It raises server utilization levels, which keeps the number of running machines low and decreases the entire energy load. Shutting down or putting standby servers to sleep also increases energy savings. Organizations benefit not only in terms of energy efficiency but also financially, as they save on operations costs such as maintenance, cooling, and real estate [13]. Research indicates that server consolidation has the potential to contribute up to 80% savings in energy in optimized environments (**Figure 8**).

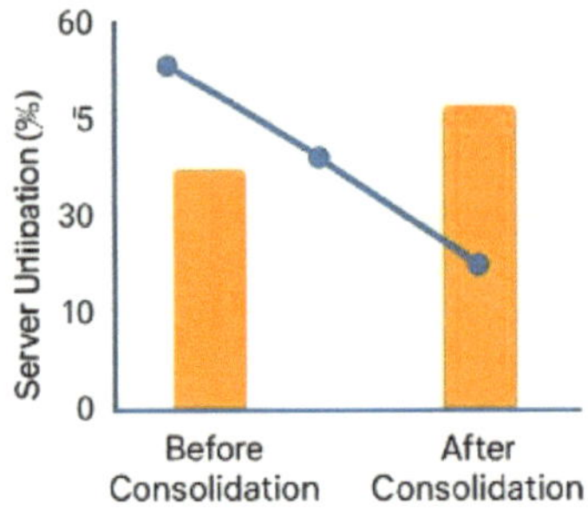

Figure 8.
Impact of server consolidation.

While valuable, server consolidation brings along resource contention, performance bottlenecks, and single points of failure. Over-consolidation can impair application performance if resource allocations are not efficiently managed. To avoid these dangers, resource scheduling has to be adaptive and dynamic to ensure workload isolation and prioritization. VM placement algorithms, real-time performance monitoring, and enforcement of quality of service (QoS) are necessary to ensure balance between consolidation and reliability of services. Server consolidation in the future is being influenced by artificial intelligence-based orchestration, forecasting with predictive analytics, and eco-friendly cloud computing [14]. Machine learning is employed to forecast workload patterns and determine guidance for proactive consolidation decisions. In addition, the use of renewable energy sources and carbon-conscious scheduling in consolidation planning increases environmental sustainability. With edge computing assuming increased importance, hybrid models integrating edge and central cloud resources are likely to enhance efficiency as well as responsiveness.

5.1.1 Hybrid models integrating edge and central cloud resources

In cloud computing, hybrid models are designed by using edge computing and centralized cloud infrastructure to ensure the best placement of workloads, faster response, and lower energy use. In the case of server consolidation, a hybrid approach lets applications be distributed between servers at the edge and those in the central data center. This way, you can put time-sensitive tasks near the user and send the rest to the cloud [13]. Reducing the need to use distant data centers for all computations is one way hybrid models help the environment. Moving data processing to the edge reduces the need for far-reaching data transmission that decreases energy expenses and network crowding [12]. In addition, servers can be gathered into fewer locations and operated with renewable sources of energy that helps lower the amount of carbon released. Such algorithms make the system more efficient by assigning tasks to the servers that use the least energy and emit the least carbon. Consolidation in hybrid models is carried out in a distributed manner [15]. Rather than only putting all workloads in one cloud, hybrid consolidation lets you gather temporary tasks at edge locations and then send them to the cloud for further processing. In some cases, edge nodes can handle initial data cleaning and send only the important data to a central system that saves both effort and storage (**Figure 9**).

This approach works well in IoT, healthcare, and industrial monitoring situations, where both quick responses and sustainability are important. Even with its positive aspects, hybrid consolidation encounters several issues: managing different types of infrastructure, dealing with performance differences, and organizing

DOI: http://dx.doi.org/10.5772/intechopen.1011479

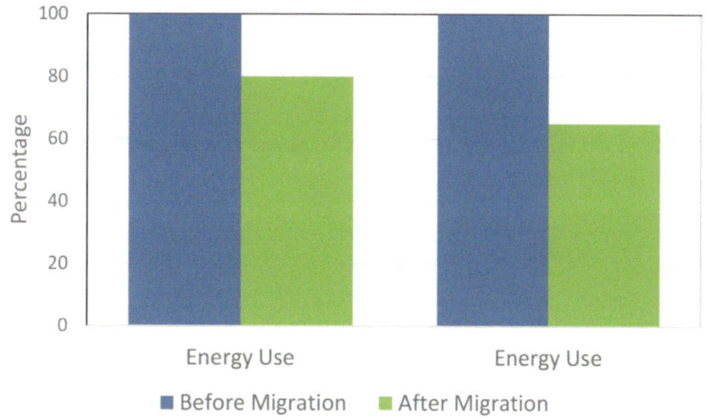

Figure 9.
Impact of load migration.

energy-conscious operations at each level [15]. Hybrid workload scheduling works best when it is aware of its environment, can predict future events, and uses powerful orchestration platforms such as Kubernetes with edge support, OpenStack, or fog computing frameworks. In addition, by matching energy use information between the edge and the cloud, it is possible to maintain sustainability goals and prevent unnecessary energy from being used. Hybrid models are expected to guide the next developments in green cloud computing (**Figure 10**).

As 5G/6G, AI and blockchain technologies develop, the edge-cloud combination will work more efficiently and on its own. More and more organizations are turning to Green AI and platforms that track energy usage in real time and modify how tasks are scheduled [16]. Hybrid consolidation, using renewable energy and smart scheduling, is a key part of building sustainable digital infrastructure today (**Figure 11**).

5.2 Load migration based on energy cost or availability

Load migration is the process of moving workloads or virtual machines (VMs) from one computing node to another using certain optimization rules. In such

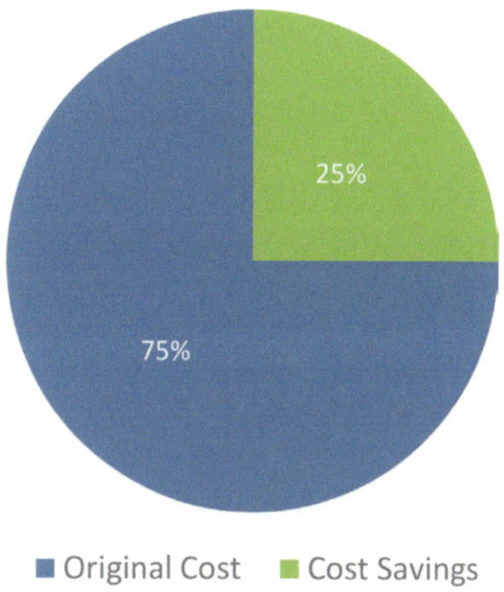

Figure 10.
Cost savings due to load migration.

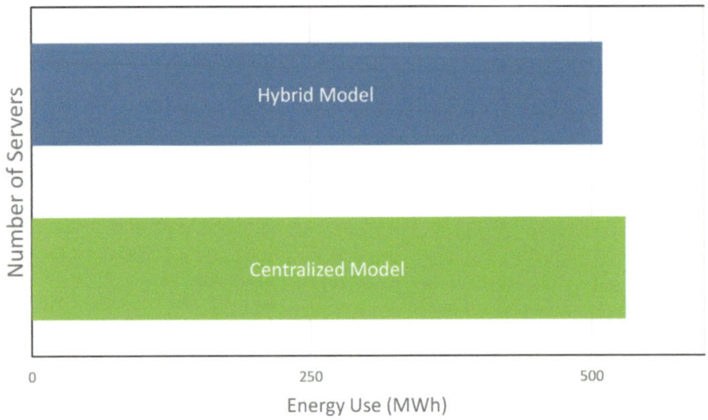

Figure 11.
Energy efficiency in hybrid vs. centralized models.

situations, energy-aware computing is mainly controlled by the cost or availability of energy, especially when solar or wind energy is not always available. Hybrid cloud designs use load migration to ensure that workloads are handled where energy is most affordable or where the greenest energy is available that helps the environment and saves money [17]. In most cases, energy-aware load migration depends on systems that track server usage, power consumption, the carbon footprint of the energy supply, and electricity prices. After that, algorithms are used to choose migration locations that require less energy or use renewable energy [11]. Hybrid models allow data processing to be moved between the center and the edge based on how much energy is available and its cost in different locations. Google and Microsoft are using smart orchestration systems to cut down on energy use during times when energy demand is highest. Hybrid architectures use energy-cost-based load migration to keep the use of edge and cloud resources balanced over time. If, for example, solar energy is plentiful at a remote edge site, some workloads can move there from the central cloud, making the system both quicker and more sustainable. Alternatively, when there is less energy, tasks can be moved to central data centers that rely more on renewable sources [18]. By using this method, you can handle more load, use energy more efficiently, and comply with local energy or carbon trading guidelines. According to research in several data centers, using energy-aware migration strategies helps reduce both carbon emissions and electricity bills. The results in the table are from a simulation-based analysis of cloud environments that uses energy-cost-aware migration policies (**Table 4**).

Moving ahead, the combination of AI-based migration, forecasting weather patterns, and real-time energy trading will guide the future of load migration. This means anticipating when renewable energy is available and when electricity tariffs will change and moving tasks ahead of time to use less energy. In addition, using blockchain for energy tracking and carbon management will allow companies to confirm that their computing is sustainable.

5.3 Time-shifting nonurgent tasks to low-energy period

Time-shifting means that you can postpone certain computing tasks to times when energy is more affordable, plentiful, or better for the environment. Batch processing, data backup, training machine learning models, and system maintenance

Scenario	Energy cost savings (%)	Carbon emission reduction (%)	Migration overhead (%)	Uptime impact (%)
No migration (baseline)	0	0	0	100
Cost-based load migration	22.5	18.7	3.2	99.6
Renewable availability-based	30.4	26.8	4.5	99.3
Hybrid cost + renewable scheduling	35.1	33.2	5	99.1

Table 4.
Performance metrics of energy-aware load migration strategies [15–17].

often use this strategy to lower peak power use and connect more with green energy. It helps ensure that both centralized and hybrid computing systems are energy efficient [18]. Time-shifting uses task classification, which means assigning urgency and service-level objectives (SLOs) to each job. Nonurgent tasks are added to a deferred queue and will be executed when energy use is low. You can achieve this by responding to signals from utility companies, using energy analytics, or using solar panels or wind turbines on your property. Important features are schedulers that consider energy use, automatic job scheduling based on time, and resource management that takes renewables into account [19]. Time-shifting brings many benefits, including less use of fossil fuels, lower energy bills, longer-lasting infrastructure, and a better match with goals for sustainability. The strategy also ensures the system does not become overloaded when there is a high demand. Especially in green data centers, time-shifting allows for a better distribution of work when renewable energy is not always available (**Table 5**).

Even though time-shifting is helpful, it introduces problems like correctly forecasting renewable energy and guaranteeing that deferred tasks stick to the SLOs. Ongoing studies are centered on using AI to make schedules, providing real-time information on the carbon intensity of the grid and using blockchain to confirm deferred task emissions [20]. As smart grids and dynamic pricing grow in use, time-shifting will probably become a main element of sustainable computing. Even though time-shifting is helpful, it introduces problems like correctly forecasting renewable energy and guaranteeing that deferred tasks stick to the SLOs. Ongoing studies are centered on using AI to make schedules, providing real-time information on the carbon intensity of the grid, and using blockchain to confirm deferred task emissions. As smart grids and dynamic pricing grow in use, time-shifting will probably become a main element of sustainable computing.

Metric	Without time-shifting	With time-shifting
Avg. energy cost per kWh (USD)	0.13	0.08
Renewable energy utilization (%)	32	58
CO_2 emissions (kg CO_2/month)	820	495
SLA compliance (%)	99.5	99.2

Table 5.
Energy and cost savings through task time-shifting [17].

6. Case study

6.1 Case study 1: Google Cloud – Carbon-aware compute scheduling

Google Cloud has introduced a plan to schedule and move nonurgent jobs to data centers that use less carbon. This method is one of many ways Google is working toward using only carbon-free energy around the clock by 2030. The system uses machine learning to determine the carbon impact of each region based on weather, energy mix, and demand, so it can schedule AI training or media processing for regions with more renewable energy. As an example, electricity use can be moved from places that rely on fossil fuels to those that use solar or wind when there is the most demand [20]. This means Google managed to lower carbon emissions from its scheduled computing by 9%, without affecting the service or its reliability. This project is linked to the goals of sustainable development for clean energy, climate action, and responsible consumption. Integrating global orchestration systems and predictive analytics into its cloud infrastructure, Google Cloud has established a new standard for energy-aware computing in the commercial cloud sector.

6.2 Case study 2: Microsoft Azure – Circular datacenter initiative

With Circular Center, Microsoft Azure is taking a new approach to sustainability by using cloud analytics and AI to help recycle and reuse data center equipment [21]. Instead of getting rid of servers that have reached the end of their useful life, Azure uses IoT and AI to find out if any parts can be fixed, given another use, or disassembled to recycle them. The insights are brought together in a cloud dashboard where you can analyze the lifecycle, monitor inventories, and decide using sustainability metrics. According to Microsoft in 2023, 83% of its data center components were reused and the remaining 17% were recycled responsibly. As a result, hardware deployment led to a 78% drop in embodied carbon emissions. In addition, the project resulted in cost savings, helped reduce e-waste, and supported Microsoft's effort to have zero-waste datacenters by 2030. By working on SDGs related to infrastructure and cities, the initiative demonstrates how cloud computing contributes to a circular economy in technology.

6.3 Case study 3: IBM cloud – Climate risk modeling for agriculture

IBM Cloud has teamed up with agricultural agencies and nongovernmental organizations in Africa and Southeast Asia to introduce a climate risk modeling platform that supports food security and environmental sustainability [16]. The system gathers weather data, satellite images, and climate history from The Weather Company to give farmers useful information through mobile and web apps. Using Watson AI and IBM Cloud, the platform predicts droughts, advises the best times to plant, and suggests irrigation plans based on water and temperature levels. In Kenya and rural India, using this model resulted in a 20–25% rise in crop yield and a 30% decrease in the amount of water used. In addition, it allowed local governments to get early alerts about climate extremes, giving them 10 days to prepare. Working toward SDGs on hunger, climate change, and land use, IBM's solution demonstrates how cloud computing can help make farming stronger against climate change and assist with social and economic growth in areas that need it (**Table 6**).

Aspect	Case Study 1: Google Cloud	Case Study 2: Microsoft Azure	Case Study 3: IBM Cloud
Initiative name	Carbon-Aware Compute Scheduling	Circular Datacentre Initiative	Climate Risk Modeling for Agriculture
Primary goal	Reduce carbon emissions from cloud workloads	Reduce e-waste and embodied carbon in hardware lifecycle	Improve agricultural resilience and food security
Core technology used	Machine learning, global workload orchestration	IoT, AI, cloud analytics, digital dashboards	Watson AI, weather forecasting, satellite imagery
Geographical focus	Global data center network	Microsoft data centers globally	Africa and Southeast Asia
Measured outcomes	9% reduction in emissions for scheduled workloads	83% reuse, 17% recycle rate; 78% drop in embodied carbon	20–25% increase in yield, 30% less water usage
Key SDGs addressed	SDG 7, SDG 12, SDG 13	SDG 9, SDG 11, SDG 12	SDG 2, SDG 13, SDG 15
Sustainability strategy	Time-shifting tasks to low-carbon regions and periods	Hardware refurbishment and life cycle extension	Data-driven decision support for climate-resilient farming
Long-term vision	24/7 carbon-free energy operations by 2030	Zero-waste data centers by 2030	Climate-smart agriculture and early warning systems

Table 6.
Comparative overview of cloud computing case studies and their sustainable impact [16, 20, 21].

7. Economic and environmental dividends

Using sustainable cloud computing helps businesses save money and protect the environment. When businesses use server virtualization, optimize their workloads, and cool their systems intelligently, they spend less on power and upkeep for their infrastructure. At large scales, these savings allow both cloud companies and businesses to invest in new ideas and grow their services in a sustainable way [20]. Practices such as using renewables, reducing emissions in data centers, and using circular IT help cut the company's carbon footprint. Thanks to this dual benefit, organizations can follow the rules, focus on sustainability, improve their image, and earn the trust of stakeholders that leads to lasting value and strength in today's digital market.

7.1 Lessening the amount of carbon emissions

A major advantage of using green cloud computing is the measurable drop in carbon emissions. Most of the electricity used by traditional data centers is still produced from fossil fuels. Green cloud practices, for example, energy-aware workload scheduling, using renewables, and consolidating virtual machines, help reduce how much energy is used and therefore help the environment [22]. It has been reported by the industry that using sustainable practices in the cloud can help providers reduce their carbon emissions by up to 80%. Additional improvements such as dynamic cooling, AI-powered energy control, and carbon-focused load balancing help make systems more efficient. They help an organization meet global climate targets and also help it look better to investors and stakeholders, as ESG is important to them (**Figure 12**).

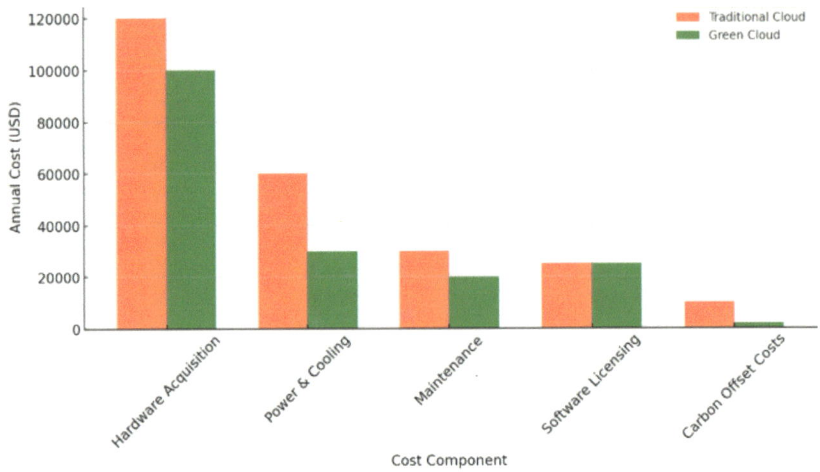

Figure 12.
TCO comparison: traditional vs. green cloud.

7.2 Reducing operational cost

Economically, green cloud computing helps companies save a lot over time by reducing their operational costs. Electricity costs, cooling charges, and unused hardware are common problems for traditional data centers. Green cloud providers reduce these problems by choosing energy-saving servers, organizing resources well through virtualization, and automating tasks [19]. As a result, energy use is lowered, hardware is used more efficiently and the need for infrastructure upgrades is reduced. As a consequence, organizations can cut down on their Total Cost of Ownership (TCO). In addition, cloud companies such as Amazon Web Services and Microsoft Azure offer discounts to customers who use less energy. In time, the energy savings and maintenance help enterprises with changing or unpredictable computing needs achieve a better return on investment (ROI).

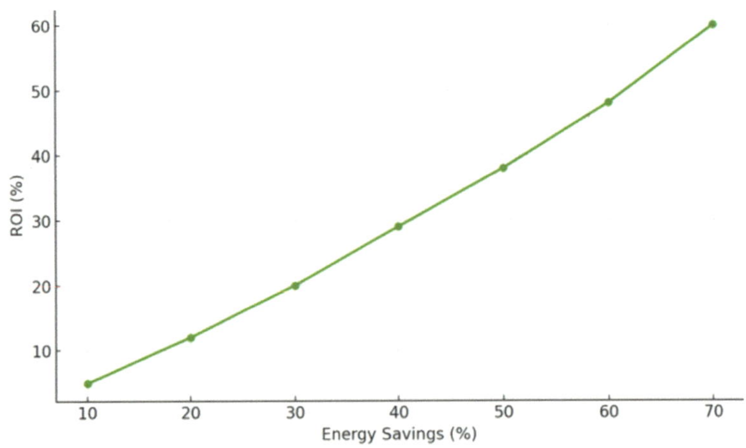

Figure 13.
ROI vs. energy savings in green cloud deployments.

7.3 Scalability vs. sustainability trade-offs

Even though scalability is a key benefit of cloud computing, making it sustainable is not easy. If scaling happens quickly, it can cause energy surges, damage hardware, and add to environmental problems if green practices are not used. Now, cloud systems use smart orchestration and containerization to manage scaling, so they can add more resources as needed without wasting resources [21]. By processing data at the edge, edge computing helps relieve this pressure by cutting down on delays and the need to expand data centers all the time. Still, businesses should approach scalability wisely, as going too big without planning can cause them to use more resources or release more carbon [23]. That is why the main focus should be on systems that can grow with demand, are energy-efficient, and use AI and predictive analytics to manage performance. Thus, organizations can make sure they do not harm the environment while growing (**Figure 13**).

8. Challenges and ethical considerations

Even though green cloud computing brings economic and environmental gains, it also creates some ethical and practical problems. A main problem is that there is no standard way to measure energy efficiency and carbon footprint among different providers. Besides, data sovereignty and privacy issues can happen when workloads are moved to places with cheaper energy or more renewables, since this could mean sending sensitive data beyond a country's borders [24]. Adding AI to energy-aware systems raises issues related to bias in algorithms and how clear the decision-making process is. Even though circular strategies often deal with e-waste, the unequal availability of recycling facilities globally makes this an ongoing issue [5]. It is important for organizations to weigh their efficiency against their social responsibility so that cost cuts do not result in job loss or unfair treatment of regions with weak laws. Therefore, businesses should focus on legal rules, protecting the environment, and engaging their stakeholders.

9. Limitations and policy directions

Even though sustainable cloud computing is promising, there are still some barriers that stop it from being fully used and effective. A major problem is that renewable energy is not always available in every region, so it is hard to use carbon-aware scheduling everywhere [22]. Regions where most energy comes from fossil fuels cannot use green computing strategies to their full potential. Virtualization and the movement of workloads from one machine to another can slow down real-time applications and increase latency. Because energy use is not always visible at the tenant level, it is hard to accurately track and manage energy efficiency in multi-tenant environments. Many organizations, especially SMEs, are held back from using green cloud solutions because upgrading their old systems is too expensive [5]. Moreover, since there are no standard sustainability benchmarks, the implementation of green cloud services is not well coordinated, which reduces their effectiveness. For sustainable cloud computing to move forward, it is important to have clear and enforceable policies. Authorities and international organizations should decide on standard ways to measure cloud sustainability, for example, by looking at carbon accounting, energy efficiency (PUE) and water efficiency (WUE) [25]. Using tax credits or carbon trading can help data centers choose renewable energy and more energy-efficient technologies. It is necessary to have rules that make cloud service providers reveal their environmental impact. In general, policies should support green IT research funding, encourage public and private groups to work together on renewable energy, and help developing countries strengthen their green infrastructure [26]. It is important for data governance and data localization rules to adapt so that environmental protection, privacy, and national security are all considered. When policy and technology are in agreement, stakeholders can create a digital future that is accessible to all, sustainable and can be expanded.

10. Future research directions

In the future, research in sustainable cloud computing ought to concentrate on developing frameworks that automatically manage workloads according to both energy supply and sustainability targets. We are seeing a rise in the need for scheduling models that are aware of carbon and that can be used with renewable energy grids to improve how and when computing tasks are done [27]. Furthermore, examining hybrid cloud-edge architectures is important, especially to see how edge computing helps lower latency and energy consumption for important applications. Studies should be conducted on using blockchain to track carbon credits and cloud resources that will make the process more transparent and responsible [28]. Another field with potential is the growth of bio-inspired cooling and quantum computing that could greatly improve energy efficiency [29]. It is important that future studies use a combination of computer science, environmental engineering, and policy analysis to handle the technical and regulatory issues in sustainable computing.

11. Summary

Transitioning to sustainable cloud computing is a necessary shift—not just a technology shift, but a shift to an opportunity, one that requires our firm commitment to best practices in order for resilience in both purpose and fiscal viability. The “business” upside in server consolidation is that organizations can improve resource utilization, modularize and tier-out redundant hardware, and optimize energy use *via* lower utilization on increasing hardware. In fact, the right practices in a hybrid environment can result in energy utilization reductions of over 80%. Adding both edge routing and edge computing into the general utility computing mix will make the entire systems processing even more responsive when coordinating among both centralized and edge-resource resourcing to sustain the responsiveness of the engagement as a function of the eventual volume of the IoT implementation. AE, in the implementation of energy-aware load migration, is the strongest option for accommodating the existence of both available and immediate energy in a contextually aligned work allocation. AE in load migratory contingencies permits the maximum utility of green energy resources for operations, with minimal carbon footprint impact to others and coupling the costs of opportunity and execution, at deeper hierarchical layers, from a collaborative ordinative perspective in a dynamic, energy-context aware manner. The simulations evidence that hybrids in migration of resources can save over 35% of energy as a cost and emissions reductions of over 33%, without adversely affecting overall system uptime on expected availability.

DOI: http://dx.doi.org/10.5772/intechopen.1011479

Moreover, shifting of tasks defined as nonessential at the margin, temporally, against external or extended peaks can provide support to both grid stability and conscious clean-source energy, and will lower average energy costs on a cost per kWh and CO_2 emissions basis while sustaining good SLA compliance as demonstrated in multiple deployments. And whether the aggregate quantifiable metric factor or cost relevancy changes, the value adds as coordinated, as a function of the model, patterns reveal the introduction to a solid transition, deploying a sustainable cloud computing system. Subsequently, server consolidation, hybrid workload management, energy-driven load migration, and time-shifting become the backbone of modern and sustainable digital infrastructure. As cloud ecosystems mature, organizations' sustainability will incorporate AI-based forecasting, intelligent orchestration platforms, and energy traceability through blockchain. Organizations must also begin to align their infrastructure decisions with their environmental priorities. By adopting these technologies, organizations can achieve carbon-aware, fiscally sustainable, and future-relevant cloud computing ecosystems.

Author details

Niyas Ahamed Sirajudeen[1*], C.S. Sree Thayanandeswari[2] and Abdul Malik Maheen[1]

1 Independent Researcher, Tamil Nadu, India

2 PET Engineering College, Tamil Nadu, India

*Address all correspondence to: niyas.ece@gmail.com

References

[1] Lopez-Vargas A, Ledezma A, Bott J, Sanchis A. Iot for global development to achieve the United Nations sustainable development goals: The new scenario after the Covid-19 pandemic. IEEE Access. 2021;**9**:124711-124726

[2] Mustapha UF, Alhassan AW, Jiang DN, Li GL. Sustainable aquaculture development: A review on the roles of cloud computing, internet of things and artificial intelligence (CIA). Reviews in Aquaculture. 2021;**13**(4):2076-2091

[3] De Villiers C, Kuruppu S, Dissanayake D. A (new) role for business–promoting the United Nations' sustainable development goals through the internet-of-things and blockchain technology. Journal of Business Research. 2021;**131**:598-609

[4] Goyal S, Agrawal A, Sergi BS. Social entrepreneurship for scalable solutions addressing sustainable development goals (SDGs) at BoP in India. Qualitative Research in Organizations and Management: An International Journal. 2021;**16**(3/4):509-529

[5] Kommisetty PDNK, Nishanth A. AI Driven Enhancements in Cloud Computing: Exploring the Synergies of Machine Learning and Generative AI. International Advanced Research Journal in Science, Engineering and Technology (Tejass Publishers). 2024;**9**(10):120-134

[6] Robles-Gómez A, Tobarra L, Pastor-Vargas R, Hernández R, Haut JM. Analyzing the users' acceptance of an IoT cloud platform using the UTAUT/TAM model. IEEE Access. 2021;**9**:150004-150020

[7] Wiryasaputra R, Huang CY, Lin YJ, Yang CT. An IoT real-time potable water quality monitoring and prediction model based on cloud computing architecture. Sensors (Basel, Switzerland: MDPI). 2024;**24**(4):1180

[8] Ma Z, Chen J, Yuan Y, Xu T. The impact of the internet of everything on green cloud computing. In: International Conference on Internet of Everything. Cham: Springer Nature Switzerland; 2024. pp. 3-11

[9] Tirlangi S, Teotia S, Padmapriya G, Kumar SS, Dhotre S, Boopathi S. Cloud computing and machine learning in the green power sector: Data management and analysis for sustainable energy. In: Developments Towards Next Generation Intelligent Systems for Sustainable Development. Hershey, PA, USA: IGI Global; 2024. pp. 148-179

[10] Thota RC. Comparative analysis of hypervisor performance: VMware vs. AWS nitro in cloud computing. International Journal of Innovative Research and Creative Technology. 2025;**11**(1):1-14

[11] Saraswat JK, Choudhari S. Integrating big data and cloud computing into the existing system and performance impact: A case study in manufacturing. Technological Forecasting and Social Change. 2025;**210**:123883

[12] Wang Y, Yang X. Machine learning-based cloud computing compliance process automation. arXiv preprint (Ithaca, NY, USA: Cornell University Library). 2025;**25**(2):163-180

[13] Lai TY, Hsu IC. Integrating semantic web into context-aware mobile application based on cloud computing. Journal of Cloud Computing. 2025;**14**(1):8

[14] Hoosain MS, Paul BS, Ramakrishna S. The impact of 4IR digital technologies and circular thinking on the United Nations sustainable development goals. Sustainability. 2020;**12**(23):10143

[15] Saxena D, Swain SR, Kumar J, Patni S, Gupta K, Singh AK, et al. Secure resource management in cloud computing: Challenges, strategies and meta-analysis. IEEE Transactions on Systems, Man, and Cybernetics: Systems, (in press). 2025. pp. 1-16

[16] Andreoli R, Mini R, Skarin P, Gustafsson H, Harmatos J, Abeni L, et al. A multi-domain survey on time-criticality in cloud computing. IEEE Transactions on Services Computing. Preprint. 2025. pp. 1-19

[17] Peter O, Mbohwa C. New future for sustainability and industrial development: Success in blockchain, internet of production, and cloud computing technology. In: 9th International Conference on Operations and Supply Chain Management, Vietnam. 2019

[18] Gahane S, Verma P. The process of encryption and decryption mechanism of data for security using cloud computing service model. In: AIP Conference Proceedings. Vol. 3227(1). Melville, NY, USA: AIP Publishing LLC; Mar 2025. p. 060014

[19] Hayyolalam V, Özkasap Ö. CBWO: A novel multi-objective load balancing technique for cloud computing. Future Generation Computer Systems. 2025;**164**:107561

[20] Wang Y, Yang X. Research on Enhancing Cloud Computing Network Security using Artificial Intelligence Algorithms. arXiv preprint arXiv:2502.17801. Ithaca, NY, USA: Cornell University Library; 2025. pp. 1-13

[21] Airaj M. Cloud computing technology and PBL teaching approach for a qualitative education in line with SDG4. Sustainability. 2022;**14**(23):15766

[22] Wang Y, Zhu M, Yuan J, Wang G, Zhou H. The Intelligent Prediction and Assessment of Financial Information Risk in the Cloud Computing Model. arXiv preprint arXiv:2404.09322. 2024. pp. 1-15

[23] Gupta R. Evaluating the contribution of CSR in achieving UN's sustainable development goals. Amity Journal of Corporate Governance. 2019;**4**(1):43-59

[24] Islam A, Anum K, Dwidienawati D, Wahab S, Abdul Latiff A. Building a post COVID-19 configuration between internet of things (IoT) and sustainable development goals (SDGs) for developing countries. Journal of Arts & Social Sciences. 2020;**4**(1):45-58

[25] Dahiya S. Harnessing cloud computing for enterprise solutions: Leveraging Java for scalable, reliable cloud architectures. Integrated Journal of Science and Technology. London, UK: Integrated Journal of Science and Technology; 2024;**1**(8):1-8

[26] Li H, Wang X, Feng Y, Qi Y, Tian J. Driving Intelligent IoT Monitoring and Control Through Cloud Computing and Machine Learning. arXiv preprint arXiv:2403.18100. 2024. pp. 1-14

[27] Akinbolaji TJ. Advanced integration of artificial intelligence and machine learning for real-time threat detection in cloud computing environments. Iconic Research and Engineering Journals. 2024;**6**(10):980-991

[28] Ryan M, Antoniou J, Brooks L, Jiya T, Macnish K, Stahl B. The ethical

balance of using smart information systems for promoting the United Nations' sustainable development goals. Sustainability. 2020;**12**(12):4826

[29] Rehan H. Revolutionizing America's cloud computing the pivotal role of AI in driving innovation and security. Journal of Artificial Intelligence General science (JAIGS). 2024;**2**(1):239-240. ISSN: 3006-4023

Chapter 2

Capacity Planning of Cloud Computing Workloads

Carlos Diego Cavalcanti Pereira

Abstract

Capacity planning in cloud computing systems is a fundamental yet evolving discipline within software engineering. As cloud-native architectures and distributed workloads increase in complexity and scale, conventional planning models—typically reactive and reliant exclusively on historical usage—are inadequate to satisfy performance, scalability, and cost-efficiency requirements. This chapter examines the theoretical underpinnings of capacity planning, elucidating the interplay between workload dynamics, software architecture, and resource management strategies. Based on a thorough literature analysis, the work delineates the primary types of planning approaches—historical, synthetic, and predictive—and rigorously evaluates their advantages and disadvantages. Significant focus is directed toward the disparity between architectural design and planning models, illustrating how the absence of integration results in inefficiencies and overprovisioning. The chapter suggests a progressive approach utilizing architecture-aware, feedback-driven models that integrate design intent, workload semantics, and real-time telemetry into cohesive capacity planning frameworks. These models seek to facilitate proactive, robust, and sustainable infrastructure techniques for contemporary cloud environments.

Keywords: cloud computing, capacity planning, software architecture, workload modeling, resource forecasting, machine learning, elasticity, performance engineering, system scalability, predictive models

1. Introduction

Cloud computing refers to the utilization of computational resources inside an environment that abstracts infrastructure, enabling scalable, on-demand access to services [1]. This approach employs cost management through operational cycles and pay-as-you-go platforms [2], providing elasticity and flexibility for applications. Engineering limits constrain cloud-based systems, despite their apparent availability of computational capacity. An essential element is capacity planning capability; it is essential for ensuring that workloads obtain adequate resources despite fluctuating operational conditions [3].

Capacity planning is particularly relevant in software engineering, as it is directly associated with software architecture [4]. The decision of architectural style—whether monolithic, microservices, or serverless—impacts the extent and nature of resource use [4]. The ISO/IEC 9126 standard defines software as a collection of computer programs, procedures, rules, and associated documentation, categorizing software quality into six essential attributes: functionality, reliability, efficiency, usability, maintainability, and portability—each influencing or being influenced by capacity planning decisions [3, 5, 6].

Furthermore, capacity planning relates to both functional attributes and non-functional criteria, including performance, availability, and durability [7–9]. In cloud-based systems, resource allocation algorithms must account for a combination of architectural patterns, anticipated demand levels, and project-specific constraints such as budget [10, 11]. A crucial factor is the accuracy of capacity planning models, which must reliably predict the requisite computing resources with a measurable level of confidence [12]. Confidence intervals are essential in this estimation, facilitating trade-offs between overprovisioning and underutilization [12, 13].

Nevertheless, this is not an elementary process. The inherent diversity of cloud workloads, along with operational uncertainties—such as hardware failures or scheduled maintenance—makes capacity planning a technical and strategic challenge [13]. The lack of overprovisioning increases the risk of resource shortages, while excessive provisioning increases costs and environmental impacts [14].

Conventional methods of capacity planning, formulated for physical infrastructure [3, 6], are frequently regarded as too inflexible or exaggerated when utilized in the dynamic contexts of modern cloud platforms [3]. In constantly evolving sectors that require agile delivery and rapid iteration, efficient and precise forecasting models are essential elements of a robust software engineering pipeline [15, 16].

In modern practice, capacity planning frequently relies on previous usage patterns to forecast future resource requirements [3, 6, 15]. This method is effective for stable systems but is inadequate in innovation-driven environments lacking prior usage data, such as new product launches or disruptive workloads [10, 16, 17]. Furthermore, dependence on historical data neglects architectural subtleties: inadequately built structures might result in inefficient resource utilization, distorting the predictions of these models [5, 18, 19].

Inefficient architectures or poorly defined functional features can produce performance artifacts that skew planning outputs from the outset [19]. The absence of clear accuracy evaluation in the majority of historical-data-based models exacerbates this issue, rendering the trustworthiness of their predictions difficult to ascertain [19]. Consequently, capacity forecasting becomes progressively subjective in fresh or intricate situations [20].

This chapter examines the present state of capacity planning for cloud computing workloads, demonstrates major shortcomings in traditional methodologies, and proposes strategies and viewpoints designed to enhance accuracy, flexibility, and sustainability in contemporary computing environments.

2. Background and theoretical foundations

Capacity planning in cloud computing environments combines multiple fundamental disciplines in software and systems engineering. This section examines five critical domains: the classification and specification of software requirements, the categorization of software systems, the principles of software architecture, the foundations of cloud computing, and the technical issues associated with capacity planning. These topics offer the crucial structure needed to comprehend how workload behavior, system architecture, and infrastructure models influence resource planning strategies.

2.1 Functional and nonfunctional requirements

In software engineering, a requirement is defined as a condition or capability necessary for a user to address an issue or attain a purpose [6]. Requirements are typically classified into functional and nonfunctional classes. Functional requirements delineate the specific services, workflows, regulations, and behaviors of a system. They outline what the system must accomplish and encompass aspects such as

- business rules and logic flows;
- system outputs and reports;
- data handling operations;
- user permissions and interactions; and
- regulatory compliance needs.

In contrast, nonfunctional requirements (NFRs) delineate the way in which the system should operate while executing its functions. These encompass attributes like performance, security, reliability, and scalability. These are frequently referred to as quality characteristics, quality objectives, restrictions, or technical specifications [21]. Their importance is sometimes undervalued in the first phases of projects, despite their substantial influence on architecture, operational expenses, and resource utilization.

Architecturally significant requirements (ASRs) primarily result from nonfunctional requirements (NFRs) [22]. Requirements like high availability or throughput limitations require meticulous capacity provisioning and infrastructure design. NFRs can be further classified into categories such as performance, operational, and efficiency criteria, each being related to resource allocation decisions [23].

Establishing specific targets according to these parameters—such as a response time of 500 milliseconds or an availability rate of 99.99%—translates them into measurable capacity demands [3]. To put the aforementioned into perspective, consider a system that requires sub-second latency during peak loads and must be able to manage worst-case scenarios rather than just average loads. Nonfunctional requirements (NFRs) are not exclusively qualitative assertions; they drive architectural decisions and affect cost.

2.2 Software classification

Software classification facilitates the generalization and comparison of systems beyond their specific context. A hierarchical classification of software into application software, system software, and programming tools has been proposed [24]. Application software includes general-purpose tools such as word processors and specialized systems like ERP or CRM. System software underlies fundamental operations and resource management, whereas programming tools enable the development of software.

However, these technical classifications may prove inadequate in real-world business scenarios. Domain-centric classification systems that correspond with user processes and operational environments are recommended [22]. Examples include the following:

- *ERP systems*: for enterprise-wide resource planning;
- *CRM platforms*: for managing customer relationships;
- *MES systems*: for managing manufacturing execution; and
- *e-commerce platforms*: for digital marketplaces.

This classification facilitates stakeholders in evaluating application resource behavior across a functional context. CRM systems typically produce substantial I/O calls and session concurrency, while MES systems prioritize real-time control and low-latency communication with hardware. These operational distinctions are essential for forecasting capacity requirements.

Determining whether a system is transactional, batch-based, real-time, or event-driven is crucial for capacity planning and influences provisioning decisions. Pressman [6] argues that integrating workload patterns with functional classifications can enhance the precision of system sizing and testing methodologies.

2.3 Software architecture

Software architecture defines the structural framework of a system and manages the interactions among its components. Software architecture consists of essential decisions on structure, communication, deployment, and quality attributes [25]. Key architectural attributes—commonly referred to as the "-ilities"—encompass scalability, availability, modifiability, and performance.

An architectural concern is considered substantial when it:

- involves design factors that extend beyond domain logic;
- affects system architecture or component interrelations; and
- it is essential to the application's success [25].

Architectural styles are typically classified into monolithic and distributed categories. Monolithic systems, while easier to manage, face challenges with scalability and fault tolerance. Distributed systems—such as microservices, service-oriented architecture, and event-driven architecture, facilitate horizontal scaling but create complexities in orchestration and consistency [25].

Sun Microsystems' "*fallacies of distributed computing*" [25] caution against erroneous assumptions, including zero latency, boundless bandwidth, and homogeneous networks. These fallacies must be confronted while architecting scalable systems, particularly in cloud contexts. Every nonfunctional criterion might influence architectural choices: high dependability necessitates replication; low latency prompts the use of edge computing or caching layers. Moreover, Conway's Law asserts that organizational structure frequently reflects system design. Consequently, architectural decisions are inherently sociotechnical, as organizational restrictions influence modularity, dependency management, and interface granularity [25].

It is crucial to emphasize that each major architectural decision influences runtime behavior, testability, and scalability [26]. Decisions about data sharing, communication protocols, or integration layers significantly impact the necessary computational and infrastructural support, hence underscoring the strong relationship between architecture and capacity planning.

2.4 Capacity planning

While capacity planning is essential in conventional infrastructure management, it is yet insufficiently developed in cloud-native contexts [6–8]. It involves estimating resource requirements to meet performance goals under projected workloads.

Aligning resource provisioning with empirical patterns of usage is crucial [27]. Nevertheless, various current approaches remain fragmented and domain-specific [28], consequently limiting generalization.

Capacity planning fundamentally represents a computationally complex problem, frequently conceptualized as a variant of the bin-packing problem—an NP-hard problem within computational complexity theory, as seen in **Figure 1**.

The intent is to arrange workloads, defined as items, into a certain number of resource containers, or bins, to reduce waste or enhance efficiency. NP-hardness, or nondeterministic polynomial-time hardness, defines problems that are at least as difficult as the most complex problems in the NP class, indicating they cannot be resolved in polynomial time and are generally addressed through decision-based formulations—such as determining whether a given amount of items can fit within a certain amount of bins, as presented in Eq. (1).

$$\begin{gathered}\text{Given}: S=\{s_1, s_2,\ldots,s_n\}, C\in\mathbb{R}^{+}, k\in\mathbb{N}\\ \text{Decide if there exists a partition of } \mathit{Sintok} \text{ or fewer bins such that}\\ \sum\nolimits_{s_i\in bin_j} s_i \le C \text{ for } \mathit{all}\ j=1,\ldots,k\end{gathered} \tag{1}$$

Eq. (1) Decision-based formulation of the bin-packing problem: given a set of workloads S, a bin capacity C, and a maximum number of bins k, the problem is to decide whether S can be partitioned into k or fewer bins such that the total size in each bin does not exceed C—capturing its NP-hard nature.

In cloud computing, this complexity increases due to circumstances such as VM-packing, where shared memory areas create interdependencies that further limit resource allocation [30]. Due to these issues, precise solutions are frequently impractical at scale, prompting practitioners to utilize approximation methods and heuristics to develop effective, although not always ideal, provisioning strategies.

A prominent example is Google's "Intention-Based Capacity Planning," a model [17] that presents a declarative approach for capacity planning. Service owners articulate their resource requirements through intent expressions rather than depending exclusively on historical facts. The model then transforms these into provisioning activities. Nonetheless, the model has limitations:

- It relies on subjective and possibly overestimated assertions.
- It fails to evaluate architectural inefficiencies.
- It grapples with unanticipated workloads devoid of historical precedence.

The challenge persists for systems that connect the abstraction of intent with the actual behavior and performance limitations of systems. Sampson et al. [31] emphasize

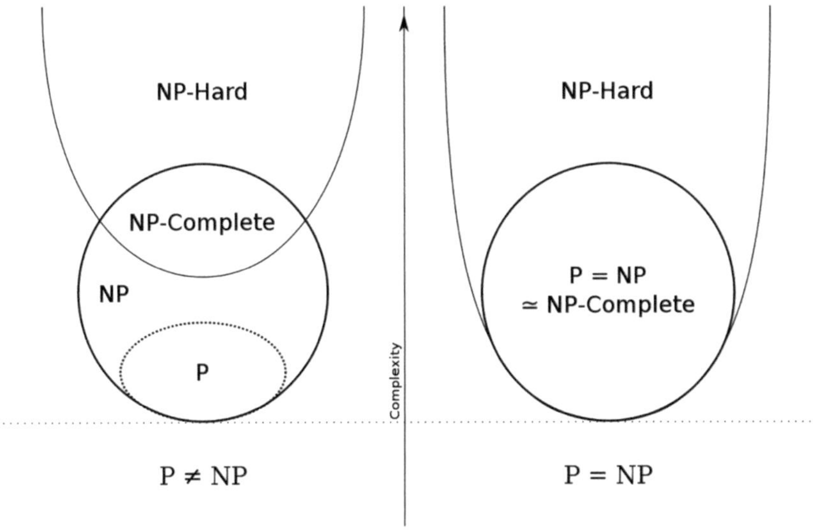

Figure 1.
Euler diagrams for P, NP, NP-complete, and NP-hard sets of problems. The left side is valid under the assumption that P ≠ NP, while the right side is legitimate under the assumption that P = NP (except that the empty language and its complement are never NP-complete) [29].

that approximation techniques, such as approximate computing, provide a means to address uncertainty in capacity planning by loosening assurances in noncritical domains.

3. Cloud capacity planning

Capacity planning in cloud environments entails the formulation of techniques and models that enable systems to predict, allocate, and oversee computing resources to ensure application performance, system scalability, and operational efficiency. In contrast to conventional infrastructures, where resource allocation typically adheres to established patterns dictated by fixed hardware capacities, cloud platforms present new complexities—such as elasticity, diverse workloads, abstraction layers, and cost-driven provisioning models—that render effective capacity planning a dynamic challenge.

3.1 Overview of the planning process

The capacity planning process in cloud environments generally includes five interrelated steps:

1. *Workload characterization*: involves comprehending the computational profile of applications, including processing cycles, memory demands, network activity, and storage input/output.

2. *Demand forecasting*: involves predicting resource utilization over time, influenced by business growth, seasonal variations, or event-induced surges.

3. *Simulation and modeling*: employing performance models to assess system behavior under fluctuating loads.

4. *Provisioning strategy*: establishing policies for scalability, auto-scaling triggers, resource allocation limits, and fallback mechanisms.

5. *Monitoring and evaluation*: ongoing assessment of resource usage and adjustments to provisioning strategies based on empirical performance.

This process is optimally perceived as a cyclical, adaptive mechanism rather than a linear process. Each phase influences and modifies the others. Telemetry from monitoring should enhance demand projections; architectural modifications should revise modeling assumptions, and cost variations should affect provisioning thresholds [32].

This five-step capacity planning approach, when correctly implemented, enhances cloud environments by increasing resilience, optimizing cost control, and improving service reliability. The absence of defined techniques throughout these stages and the insufficient integration of architectural concepts represent notable deficiencies in the current state of the art [33, 34].

3.2 Capacity planning approaches

The scientific literature offers various methodological approaches for planning the capacity of cloud computing use cases. These methodologies are generally structured around three primary strategies: (i) models derived from historical usage, (ii) simulation and synthetic benchmarking, and (iii) prediction models utilizing machine learning techniques. Each has unique advantages and limitations, with their relevance contingent upon workload characteristics, data accessibility, and architectural sophistication [35].

3.2.1 Models derived from historical usage

These models depend on the retrospective analysis of resource utilization to predict future demand [36]. They are extensively utilized because of their minimal implementation complexity and dependence on data previously gathered by cloud monitoring systems. Common measurements encompass CPU and memory usage, disk throughput, and request frequencies. They are especially efficacious for mature, steady workloads with well-defined operating baselines.

Nevertheless, these models encounter considerable constraints when utilized for innovative or unstable workloads. They presume that future demand will mirror historical usage patterns, an assumption that falters in scenarios characterized by rapid scaling, architectural transformation, or unusual usage patterns. In scenarios marked by innovation or disruption, this reactive approach often fails to anticipate changes in consumption trends [33, 34].

3.2.2 Simulation and synthetic benchmarking

Synthetic benchmarking is frequently employed to simulate anticipated performance in the absence of previous data, such as in greenfield development or replatforming situations [35]. The process may entail replicating traffic patterns, doing specified stress tests, or utilizing benchmarking suites that emulate user behavior in controlled environments. Simulation tools can examine edge cases, verify scaling policies, and assess infrastructure performance under load.

Synthetic models, however beneficial in planning or testing phases, generally do not encapsulate the complete intricacy of actual production situations. They may overlook network unpredictability, user behavior diversity, or inter-service latency. Consequently, they frequently generate idealized performance predictions that are either optimistic or unduly cautious upon implementation [33, 34].

3.2.3 Prediction models utilizing machine learning techniques

An important segment of capacity planning research investigates machine learning (ML) to predict resource requirements. These models utilize historical logs, runtime measurements, or architectural features to generate dynamic, adaptive forecasts. Prevalent methodologies encompass time-series forecasting (ARIMA, LSTM), clustering, regression trees, and reinforcement learning for policy enhancement [37].

Machine learning methodologies exhibit significant adaptability and have the capability to identify subtle patterns or anomalies that conventional models may neglect. However, machine learning models are significantly reliant on the quantity and quality of training data. They also present operational problems, including the necessity for model retraining, versioning, and explainability—particularly when capacity decisions affect business-critical systems [33, 34].

Numerous predictive models are challenging to audit, impeding their implementation in contexts that necessitate transparency and traceability in decision-making.

3.2.4 Comparative landscape

The **Table 1** delineates the three predominant techniques, emphasizing their respective strengths, limitations, and optimal applications.

3.2.5 Architectural awareness in existing models

A significant constraint across all categories is the inadequate incorporation of architectural context into planning rationale. Most models view the system as an opaque entity, prioritizing consumption measurements over the impact of architectural elements like microservices interactions, communication protocols, or service dependencies on resource behavior. Focusing on consumption measurements rather than architectural impacts can lead to erroneous predictions and excessive resource provisioning [33, 34].

Approach	Advantages	Limitations	Best-fit scenarios
Models derived from historical usage	Accessible, readily available data	Ineffective for innovative or fluctuating workloads	Legacy applications; fluctuating business demands
Simulation and synthetic benchmarking	Beneficial for development, consistent testing circumstances	Limited realism; deficient in behavioral diversity	Pre-deployment testing; infrastructure scaling
Prediction models utilizing machine learning techniques	Adaptive: discerns concealed patterns within extensive datasets	Demands pristine, high-volume data; constraints on explainability	IoT, event-driven systems, and dynamic traffic

Table 1.
Comparative landscape of approaches for planning cloud capacity [33].

In systems characterized by intricate service meshes or event-driven workflows, resource consumption may surge not as a result of traffic but rather due to design inefficiencies [38]. In the absence of comprehension regarding these design factors, planners frequently resort to excessive resource allocation as a precautionary measure.

In conclusion, although no singular strategy prevails, each approach offers significant mechanisms for capacity estimation across varying settings. The growing implementation of hybrid strategies—integrating historical data, simulation tools, and predictive models—signifies a movement toward more comprehensive, data-informed, and architecture-conscious capacity planning processes [33, 34].

3.3 Challenges in practice

Different models and techniques have been suggested for capacity planning in cloud computing; however, the literature identifies several persistent difficulties that limit the applicability, accuracy, and implementation of these models. These restrictions are not solely technical; they also arise from the disjointed fashion in which planning is conducted across several teams, tools, and architectural layers.

Four primary kinds of problems are particularly significant: (i) absence of standards, (ii) constraints in predicting accuracy, (iii) inadequate generalization across workload types, and (iv) cross-dimensional complexity [33, 34].

3.3.1 Absence of standards

A significant challenge is the lack of defined inputs, outputs, and procedural frameworks to conduct capacity planning. Although other models depend on analogous metrics—such as CPU utilization, request delay, memory consumption, or transaction volume—there is no standardized format or methodology for gathering, understanding, or employing this data across platforms.

This fragmentation also extends to predicting outputs. Certain models generate scalar thresholds (e.g., maximum CPU at 85%), while others provide multidimensional vectors (e.g., trade-offs among CPU, memory, and concurrent levels). The absence of a standardized vocabulary and performance metrics complicates the comparison and integration of findings across tools and teams [39].

In the absence of standardized instrumentation and telemetry, more advanced models become fragile or difficult to sustain, particularly in multicloud or hybrid environments. Without standardized instrumentation and telemetry, benchmarking and reusing best practices become challenging [33, 34].

3.3.2 Constraints in predicting accuracy

Despite models being technically accurate and effectively executed, their practical efficacy—specifically, the extent to which they can precisely forecast future resource requirements—remains constrained.

Various capacity planning methodologies depend on reactive strategies, such as threshold-based scaling, which initiate provisioning solely after a service undergoes stress. Some rely on previous usage trends but encounter difficulties when faced with unforeseen spikes, alterations in user behavior, or shifts in workload.

This issue becomes increasingly significant when managing workloads that demonstrate erratic growth patterns or show heightened sensitivity to alterations in architecture or data volume. In such instances, models may overfit historical trends, resulting in projections that are excessively conservative (causing cost inefficiency) or perilously optimistic (resulting in service degradation) [33, 34].

Furthermore, the majority of models do not explicitly measure their uncertainty or integrate error margins into their planning recommendations [40]. Consequently, they provide no framework for assessing confidence levels, which would otherwise assist engineers and business stakeholders in making risk-informed decisions.

3.3.3 Inadequate generalization across workload types

A further difficulty is the absence of universally applicable planning models that can function efficiently across various workload categories. Contemporary methodologies are frequently closely linked to particular workload categories, including IoT telemetry ingestion, web service orchestration, database queries, or data lake processing [41].

This leads to isolated solutions that are difficult to adapt to other domains without significant reengineering. A capacity model designed for managing web requests per second may not be suitable for event-driven pipelines, where latency and throughput are regulated by message brokers and asynchronous handlers.

The literature indicates that numerous models have assumptions on service behavior that are invalid beyond the initial testing settings. These assumptions are hardly recorded, complicating the adaptation of the model to diverse contexts [33, 34, 41].

This tendency toward specialization restricts reuse and elevates the operational burden of managing numerous planning models for various segments of the infrastructure. Sharing knowledge, automating policies, and enforcing uniform governance across a heterogeneous application ecosystem becomes challenging.

3.3.4 Cross-dimensional complexity

In addition, cloud systems provide a distinct layer of complexity by integrating operational, architectural, and economic factors. Capacity planning decisions must fulfill performance needs while also conforming to cost limitations, availability objectives, compliance regulations, and environmental considerations, including regional data residency [42].

Models that concentrate exclusively on technical measures, disregarding architectural relationships or financial ramifications, are frequently insufficient. However, constructing models that effectively integrate technical measures, architectural relationships, and financial ramifications continues to pose a substantial challenge in both academic and practical contexts (**Table 2**) [33, 34].

Addressing these difficulties requires more than mere algorithmic expertise. It necessitates an interdisciplinary approach that examines the intersection of cloud capacity planning with software architecture, DevOps processes, Site Reliability Engineering (SRE) methods, and business strategy.

3.4 Architecture-aware planning gaps

A notable but insufficiently examined constraint in models for planning cloud capacity is the inadequate integration of capacity forecasting methods with software architecture design. System architecture ought to be a fundamental component of any dependable capacity planning model, as it directly affects workload allocation, resource contention, delay pathways, and scaling dynamics. Research reveals that the

Challenge category	Description	Implications
Absence of standards	Lack of standardized formats for metrics, regulations, or telemetry	It is difficult to integrate tools, automate models, or conduct cross-platform comparisons
Constraints in predicting accuracy	Models frequently exhibit inaccuracies in response to architectural modifications or fluctuations in activity	Results in excessive provisioning or service instability
Inadequate generalization across workload types	Methods are limited in scope and tailored to particular domains	Necessitates the construction of new models for each category of task
Cross-dimensional complexity	Technical, architectural, and economic dimensions are frequently compartmentalized	Obstructs comprehensive and sustainable planning

Table 2.
Summary of challenges in cloud capacity planning [33].

majority of planning methodologies view the system as a mysterious entity, prioritizing consumption measurements over structural elements like component coupling, communication techniques, and deployment topologies [43].

This exclusion has significant repercussions. A microservices-based application with tightly connected services and synchronous communication may demonstrate inconsistent resource utilization due to inter-service delays or cascade failures. In such instances, capacity models may advocate for excessive provisioning to alleviate performance degradation, although the underlying problem may stem from design inefficiencies. Lacking insight into these structural patterns, capacity projections may be either exaggerated or misaligned with the real requirements of the system [33, 34, 43].

On top of that, various forms of architecture impose distinct requirements on infrastructure. Monolithic programs often exhibit consistent, centralized usage patterns, while distributed systems—particularly those employing event-driven or service-oriented architectures—introduce unpredictability in aspects like throughput, latency, and concurrency [44]. Planning models that disregard these intricacies often oversimplify behavior, resulting in erroneous provisioning strategies.

A common error is the omission of architectural restrictions and quality features in planning assumptions. Attributes like scalability, fault tolerance, availability, and security are not merely post-deployment considerations; they derive from design choices and influence a system's performance under load [45]. A system characterized by eventual consistency and loose coupling would exhibit distinct scaling properties that are different from those that rely on rigorous transactional integrity and robust inter-component coordination.

Notwithstanding these factors, few models in the literature integrate architecture-driven variables into their prediction frameworks. Aspects like service fan-out, transaction depth, orchestration versus choreography, and the use of circuit breakers or retries are infrequently quantified or modeled. This lack of quantification or modeling breaks the connection between capacity planning and architectural reasoning, forcing teams to rely on experimentation or over-engineering to meet performance goals [33, 34, 45].

The absence of architectural understanding in capacity planning fosters a reactive culture, wherein resource issues are managed operationally instead of being preemptively designed [45]. When planning is separated from architecture, scaling policies transform into fragmented solutions rather than cohesive optimizations. This approach also leads to inefficiencies in cloud expenditure, as resources are frequently allocated to address inadequate design instead of genuine need.

Future planning frameworks must explicitly incorporate architectural descriptors into their inputs and logic to overcome this gap [46]. This includes the following:

- evaluating component connections and coupling degrees for assessing inter-service overhead;
- identifying important pathways and synchronous relationships to predict bottlenecks;
- integrating architectural patterns—such as layered, hexagonal, or microkernel designs—as determinants that influence resource behavior; and
- synchronizing capacity models with quality parameters established during software design, including availability objectives and elasticity specifications.

Additionally, synchronizing architectural documentation (e.g., C4 models, ADRs) with observability platforms and planning tools might furnish a more comprehensive and contextual foundation for decision-making. Planners can incorporate design-time intent in addition to telemetry, facilitating more precise, sustainable, and proactive provisioning techniques.

The absence of architectural integration in capacity planning models constitutes a fundamental deficiency that diminishes their efficacy. To resolve this issue, planning must transition from a reactive operational function to a design-informed engineering discipline—one that regards architecture as both context and constraint [33, 34].

3.5 Toward an integrated model

To tackle the challenges and deficiencies in existing capacity planning methodologies, it is crucial to propose a new generation of models that are both adaptive and context-aware, able to integrate architectural intent, workload semantics, and operational telemetry into a cohesive planning process. Current models typically function within confined parameters: they either concentrate on usage history, employ abstract simulations, or utilize machine learning without cohesive architectural integration. Consequently, they are inadequate when utilized in contemporary, dynamic, and heterogeneous cloud-native systems.

A more effective strategy would commence with redefining the inputs to the planning process. Models should integrate workload descriptors—such as execution models (e.g., stateless APIs versus streaming jobs), anticipated concurrency levels, and essential business SLAs—alongside architectural attributes like service topologies, dependency graphs, fault domains, and communication protocols instead of relying solely on time-series resource metrics. These inputs furnish semantic context that enhances the predictive relevance of the model, especially in the absence of past usage [47].

In addition, capacity planning must transition from static forecasting to a continuous planning cycle that incorporates real-time runtime telemetry. Such information encompasses observability data, including latency, request error rates, and saturation measurements, which inform the capacity engine to verify and enhance estimations over time. Feedback loops facilitate the planning model's self-correction, allowing it to dynamically adapt to changes in usage patterns or architectural implementations [45].

The foundation of the planning model must be a capacity engine that facilitates hybrid reasoning by integrating rule-based thresholds, simulation, probabilistic models, and machine learning methodologies. This engine must be modular, enabling components to be substituted or recalibrated according to the degree of uncertainty, criticality, or data availability in each application. In contexts with little telemetry yet clearly specified architecture, simulation and domain heuristics may prevail; conversely, in high-data-volume contexts, statistical learning may be prioritized.

A comprehensive conceptual framework for this approach is illustrated in **Figure 2**:

This integrated approach facilitates provisioning decisions based on both usage projections and deliberate design considerations, a crucial capacity in architectures where resource consumption is influenced equally by structural choices and external demand. A service with extensive synchronous dependency chains may necessitate buffer capacity during peak periods, irrespective of usual traffic volumes. However, if we integrate architectural knowledge into the model, we can anticipate such patterns, which traditional forecasting approaches rarely capture.

To realize this objective, various supplementary capabilities are necessary:

- *Unified Modeling Language for capacity*: A structured method to depict workloads, architectural limitations, and resource objectives that can be utilized by planning engines and verified by stakeholders.

- *Reference workload taxonomies*: Classification frameworks that assist in recognizing planning methods based on workload characteristics, including throughput sensitivity, starting latency, or burst tolerance.

- *Mechanisms for adaptation driven by feedback*: Integration with observability and telemetry technologies to facilitate real-time performance assessment and automated optimization of provisioning policies.

- *Integration of DevOps with Site Reliability Engineering (SRE)*: Integrating capacity planning into CI/CD pipelines and service reliability frameworks helps advance the planning process earlier in the lifecycle and nearer to decision-making junctures.

By implementing these concepts, capacity planning may transition from a reactive, usage-focused activity to a design-oriented, predictive practice proficient in

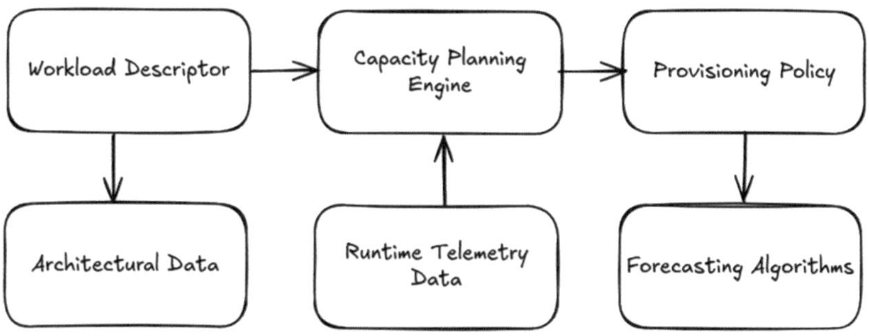

Figure 2.
High-level conceptual framework for cloud capacity planning. (Author).

supporting cloud-native designs at scale. The objective is to improve resource utilization while establishing durable, scalable systems that honor operational reality and architectural integrity [41, 42, 45].

3.6 Final considerations

Capacity planning in cloud computing has emerged as an essential component for optimizing performance, ensuring availability, and managing costs. Nonetheless, existing methodologies remain disjointed, predominantly emphasizing reactive strategies grounded in past usage data. Although efficient for stable workloads, these models encounter difficulties in situations involving novel, dynamic, or structurally intricate systems. The absence of defined inputs, outputs, and modeling procedures hinders interoperability and restricts the reutilization of models across different contexts.

A significant disparity exists in the insufficient integration between capacity planning and software architecture. Many models neglect to account for structural characteristics—such as service coupling, dependency depth, or communication protocols—that directly affect resource consumption by workloads. This disconnection frequently leads to erroneous predictions, ineffective scalability, or superfluous resource overprovisioning. A more profound integration of architectural design and planning models is essential to foresee performance limitations and foster sustainable scaling.

To overcome these restrictions, future capacity planning must transform into a more comprehensive discipline that integrates design-time information, runtime telemetry, and adaptive feedback mechanisms. Incorporating workload semantics, architectural characteristics, and performance targets into cohesive models will be crucial for accommodating progressively varied and dynamic cloud workloads. This transition will allow businesses to make more proactive, robust, and economical infrastructure decisions, even without historical antecedents.

4. Conclusions

Capacity planning in cloud computing environments has become a strategic issue, serving not only operational needs but also facilitating scalability, dependability, and cost management in digital systems. As workloads diversify and systems become more distributed, the shortcomings of conventional planning methods—initially designed for stable, predictable infrastructures—are increasingly revealed. Models reliant solely on past usage data, although beneficial in stable situations, struggle when confronted with innovation, quick expansion, or architectural modifications.

The literature indicates that current methodologies predominantly emphasize reactive tactics, concentrating on performance monitoring and threshold-based provisioning instead of proactive forecasting. Numerous models see workloads as black boxes, devoid of recognition of structural attributes like service interdependencies, concurrency patterns, or communication protocols. The lack of architectural integration frequently results in excessive provisioning choices or unexpected bottlenecks, especially in systems structured with microservices, event-driven architectures, or asynchronous messaging.

Furthermore, planning models often function within discrete domains. They are designed for particular workload categories—such as IoT telemetry, web apps, or data analytics—lacking methods for reuse or modification in other contexts. This fragmentation restricts the generalizability of findings and compels enterprises to manage capacity using a disjointed array of methods and heuristics. The absence of uniformity in inputs, outputs, and performance measures impedes interoperability and automation, hence elevating the cognitive and operational burden of capacity management.

The future of cloud capacity planning will involve the integration of architecture-aware modeling, predictive analytics, and continuous feedback systems to tackle these difficulties. Integrated models must transcend utilization measurements to encompass workload descriptors, quality features, and intentional design objectives. Integrating these components into planning engines—enhanced by real-time telemetry and adaptive algorithms—facilitates more precise demand forecasting, dynamic resource optimization, and alignment of provisioning decisions with technical limitations and business goals.

Ultimately, cloud capacity planning must transition from a reactive, infrastructure-focused approach to a proactive, multidisciplinary profession. It must connect software design with operational execution, facilitating sustainable growth, innovation, resilience, and financial accountability. As systems evolve to become increasingly intelligent and autonomous, the tactics that regulate their scalability must also advance. In this context, capacity planning transcends mere infrastructure considerations; it involves aligning design intent, performance expectations, and actual behavior through meticulous technical precision.

A. Comparative landscape of cloud capacity planning approaches

See **Table A1**.

Approach	Advantages	Limitations	Best-fit scenarios
Models derived from historical usage	Accessible, readily available data	Ineffective for innovative or fluctuating workloads	Legacy applications; fluctuating business demands
Simulation and synthetic benchmarking	Beneficial for development, consistent testing circumstances	Limited realism; deficient in behavioral diversity	Pre-deployment testing; infrastructure scaling
Prediction models utilizing machine learning techniques	Adaptive: discerns concealed patterns within extensive datasets	Demands pristine, high-volume data; constraints on explainability	IoT, event-driven systems, and dynamic traffic

Table A1.
Comparative landscape of cloud capacity planning approaches.

B. Summary of challenges in cloud capacity planning

See **Table B1**.

Challenge category	Description	Implications
Absence of standards	Lack of standardized formats for metrics, regulations, or telemetry	It is difficult to integrate tools, automate models, or conduct cross-platform comparisons
Constraints in predicting accuracy	Models frequently exhibit inaccuracies in response to architectural modifications or fluctuations in activity	Results in excessive provisioning or service instability
Inadequate generalization across workload types	Methods are limited in scope and tailored to particular domains	Necessitates the construction of new models for each category of task
Cross-dimensional complexity	Technical, architectural, and economic dimensions are frequently compartmentalized	Obstructs comprehensive and sustainable planning

Table B1.
Summary of challenges in cloud capacity planning.

Acknowledgements

I would like to express my sincere gratitude to CESAR School for its continuous academic assistance and for facilitating my active engagement in teaching and research in software engineering, distributed systems, and cloud computing. The academic atmosphere at CESAR School has been instrumental in cultivating critical reflections and facilitating multidisciplinary discussions that directly impacted the production of this work.

Special gratitude is extended to Valcann, the intersection of scientific research and practical application. This organization consistently tests and confirms theoretical ideas through empirical application. Valcann serves as a dynamic laboratory, transforming hypotheses into prototypes, while the intricacies of real-world systems propel the evolution of technical fields.

This work results from academic rigor and industry pragmatism, made possible by the interaction between these two fields.

Nomenclature

Capacity planning	The procedure of assessing the resources necessary for a system to achieve performance and availability objectives under specified workloads.
Cloud computing	Internet-based access to IT resources with consumption-based pricing structures.
Workload	A collection of operations, applications, or procedures performed by a system that utilizes computational resources.

Provisioning strategy	Protocols and systems are employed to distribute and adjust infrastructure resources in response to demand.
Telemetry	Real-time performance and utilization statistics are gathered from systems and applications.
NFR (Nonfunctional Requirement)	Systemic restrictions and quality characteristics, including performance, scalability, and security.
ASR (Architecturally Significant Requirement)	A stipulation that affects system architecture and shapes design choices.
Service mesh	An infrastructure layer specifically designed for overseeing service-to-service communication within microservices systems.
ML (Machine Learning)	A category of algorithms employed to identify patterns and provide predictions based on data.
Black box model	A model that deduces behavior exclusively from inputs and outputs, lacking understanding of internal structure.
SLA (Service-Level Agreement)	A contractual obligation that delineates the anticipated performance or availability standards of a service.

Author details

Carlos Diego Cavalcanti Pereira
CESAR School, Recife, Brazil

*Address all correspondence to: cdcp@cesar.school

References

[1] Jamshidi P, Ahmad A, Pahl C. Cloud migration research: A systematic review. IEEE Transactions on Cloud Computing. 2013;**1**(2):142-157

[2] Bhardwaj S, Jain L, Jain S. Cloud computing: A study of infrastructure as a service (IaaS). International Journal of Engineering. 2010;**2**(1):60-63

[3] Gunther NJ. Guerilla Capacity Planning: A Tactical Approach to Planning for Highly Scalable Applications and Services. 1st ed. New York, NY: Springer; 2010

[4] Bell M. Enterprise capacity planning for end-state architecture. In: Incremental Software Architecture. Hoboken, NJ: Wiley; 2016. pp. 235-252

[5] International Organization for Standardization (ISO/IEC) Software Engineering—Product Quality. ISO/IEC 9126. Geneva, Switzerland: ISO; 2001

[6] Pressman RS. Software Engineering: A Practitioner's Approach, 7th McGraw-Hill. New York, NY; 2009

[7] Ameller D et al. How do software architects consider non-functional requirements: An exploratory study. In: The 20th IEEE International Requirements Engineering Conference (RE). New York, NY: IEEE; 2012

[8] Rosa NS, Cunha PRF, Justo GRR. An approach for reasoning and refining non-functional requirements. Journal of the Brazilian Computer Society. 2004;**10**(1):62-84

[9] Byun H, Lee J, Kim M. An analytical model-based capacity planning approach for building performance-effective CSD-based compute nodes. ACM Transactions on Modeling and Performance Evaluation of Computing Systems. 2023;**8**(3):1-25. DOI: 10.1145/3623677

[10] Anupama KC, Nagaraja R, Jaiganesh M. A perspective view of resource-based capacity planning in cloud computing. In: Proceedings of the 1st International Conference on Advanced Information Technology (ICAIT). Singapore: Springer; 2019

[11] Fowler SJ. Production-Ready Microservices. Sebastopol, CA: O'Reilly; 2016

[12] Petty MD. Calculating and Using Confidence Intervals for Model Validation. 2013

[13] Carvalho M, Menascé DA, Brasileiro F. Capacity planning for IaaS cloud providers offering multiple service classes. Future Generation Computer Systems. 2017;**77**:97-111

[14] Furman E, Diamant A. Optimal capacity planning for cloud service providers with periodic, time-varying demand. European Journal of Operational Research. 2025;**322**(1):133-146. DOI: 10.1016/j.ejor.2024.11.017

[15] Amiri M, Mohammad-Khanli L. Survey on prediction models of applications for resources provisioning in cloud. Journal of Network and Computer Applications. 2017;**82**:93-113

[16] Lloyd W et al. The cloud services innovation platform—Enabling service-based environmental modeling using IaaS cloud computing. In: iEMSs 2012. Germany: iEMSs Leipzig; 2012. pp. 1208-1215

[17] Beyer B et al. Site Reliability Engineering: How Google Runs Production Systems. 1st ed. Sebastopol, CA: O'Reilly; 2016

[18] Reese G. Cloud Application Architectures. Sebastopol, CA: O'Reilly; 2009

[19] Medel V et al. Characterizing resource management performance in Kubernetes. Computers and Electrical Engineering. 2018;**68**:286-297

[20] Jung CF. Metodologia Científica: Ênfase em Pesquisa Tecnológica. São Paulo, Brazil: Érica Editora; 2003

[21] Sommerville I. Software Engineering. 10th ed. London, UK: Pearson; 2015

[22] Chen L, Babar MA, Nuseibeh B. Characterizing architecturally significant requirements. IEEE Software. 2013;**30**(2):38-45

[23] Ambler S. Technical (Non-Functional) Requirements: An Agile Introduction. Agile Modeling; 2006. [Online]. Available from: http://www.agilemodeling.com/essays/examiningBRUF.htm

[24] Abid M, Amjad M. Fundamentals of Computers. New Delhi, India: I.K. International Publishing House; 2015

[25] Richards M, Ford N. Fundamentals of Software Architecture. Sebastopol, CA: O'Reilly Media, Inc.; 2020

[26] Nygard M. Release it! Design and Deploy Production-Ready Software. Raleigh, NC: Pragmatic Bookshelf; 2007

[27] Morgan G, Harmon R. Data Collection Techniques. Journal of the American Academy of Child and Adolescent Psychiatry. 2001;**40**:973-976

[28] Jedlitschka A, Pfahl D. Reporting guidelines for controlled experiments in software engineering. In: International Symposium on Empirical Software Engineering. New York, NY: IEEE; 2005. p. 2005

[29] van Leeuwen J. Handbook of Theoretical Computer Science. Amsterdam, Netherlands: Elsevier; 1994

[30] Sindelar M, Sitaraman RK, Shenoy P. Sharing-aware algorithms for virtual machine colocation. In: Proceedings of the 23rd ACM Symposium on Parallelism in Algorithms and Architectures (SPAA). New York, NY: ACM; 2011

[31] Sampson A et al. EnerJ: Approximate data types for safe and general low-power computation. In: Proceedings of the 32nd ACM SIGPLAN Conference on Programming Language Design and Implementation. New York, NY: ACM; 2011

[32] Angelis A, Kousiouris G. A Survey on the Landscape of Self-Adaptive Cloud Design and Operations Patterns: Goals, Strategies, Tooling, Evaluation and Dataset Perspectives. 2025 arXiv preprint arXiv:2503.06705

[33] Pereira CDC, Ferraz FS. Capacity planning of cloud computing workloads: A systematic review. In: ICSEA 2020, the Fifteenth International Conference on Software Engineering Advances. Wilmington, DE: IARIA; 2020. pp. 61-67

[34] Pereira CDC. Capacity planning of cloud computing workloads [PhD thesis]. Recife, Brazil: Recife Center for Advanced Studies and Systems; 2023

[35] Sekar J. Artificial intelligence-driven predictive analytics for cloud capacity planning. IRE Journal. 2023;**7**(2):667

[36] Shaikh R, Muntean CH, Gupta S. Prediction of resource utilization in

cloud computing using machine learning. In: Proceedings of the 14th International Conference on Cloud Computing and Services Science (CLOSER 2024). Cham, Switzerland: Springer; 2024. pp. 103-114. DOI: 10.5220/0012742200003711

[37] Wang Y, Yang X. Intelligent resource allocation optimization for cloud computing via machine learning. Advances in Computer, Signals and Systems. 2025;**9**(1):55-63. DOI: 10.23977/acss.2025.090109

[38] Zhu X, She G, Xue B, Zhang Y, Zhang Y, Zou X K, et al. Dissecting overheads of service mesh sidecars. In: Proc. ACM Symposium on Cloud Computing (SoCC '23). New York, NY: ACM; 2023. pp. 142-157. DOI: 10.1145/3620678.3624652

[39] Saxena D, Kumar J, Singh AK, Schmid S. Performance analysis of machine learning centered workload prediction models for cloud. IEEE Transactions on Parallel and Distributed Systems. 2023;**34**(4):910-923. DOI: 10.1109/TPDS.2023.3240567

[40] Rossi A, Visentin A, Carraro D, Prestwich S, Brown KN. Forecasting workload in cloud computing: towards uncertainty-aware predictions and transfer learning. Cluster Computing. 2025;**28**(4):Article 258. DOI: 10.1007/s10586-024-04933-2

[41] Andreadis G, Mastenbroek F, van Beek V, Iosup A. Capelin: Data-driven compute capacity procurement for cloud datacenters using portfolios of scenarios. IEEE Transactions on Parallel and Distributed Systems. 2022;**33**(1):26-39. DOI: 10.1109/TPDS.2021.3084816

[42] Qi S, Milojicic D, Bash C, Pasricha S. MOSAIC: A multi-objective optimization framework for sustainable datacenter management. In: Proceedings of the 2023 IEEE 30th International Conference on High Performance Computing, Data, and Analytics (HiPC). New York, NY: IEEE; 2023. pp. 51-60. DOI: 10.1109/HiPC58850.2023.00046

[43] Becker S, Koziolek H, Reussner R. Capacity planning for event-based systems using automated performance prediction. In: Proceedings of the 26th IEEE/ACM International Conference on Automated Software Engineering (ASE). IEEE/ACM; 2011. pp. 125-134. DOI: 10.1109/ASE.2011.6100073

[44] Blinowski G, Ojdowska A, Przybyłek A. Monolithic vs. Microservice Architecture: A Performance and Scalability Evaluation. IEEE Access. 2022;**10**:20357-20374. DOI: 10.1109/ACCESS.2022.3152803

[45] Lichtenthäler R, Fritzsch J, Wirtz G. Cloud-native architectural characteristics and their impacts on software quality: A validation survey. In: Proceedings of the 2023 IEEE International Conference on Service-Oriented System Engineering (SOSE). New York, NY: IEEE; 2023. pp. 9-18. DOI: 10.1109/SOSE58276.2023.00008

[46] Rosinosky G, Schmitz D, Rivière E. StreamBed: Capacity planning for stream processing. In: Proceedings of the 18th ACM International Conference on Distributed and Event-Based Systems (DEBS '24). New York, NY: ACM; 2024. pp. 90-102. DOI: 10.1145/3653531.3653542

[47] Wen L, Xu M, Toosi AN, Ye K. TempoScale: A cloud workloads prediction approach integrating short-term and long-term information. In: Proceedings of the 2024 IEEE 17th International Conference on Cloud Computing (CLOUD). New York, NY: IEEE; 2024. pp. 183-193. DOI: 10.1109/CLOUD62652.2024.00030

Chapter 3

Perspective Chapter: Trusted and Intelligent Cloud Computing for Logistics Industry Alliance

Deqian Fu, Yaxian Jing, Ziqi Liu, Zhanling Shi, Zanmei Wu, Jinze Ma and Qianhui Ma

Abstract

In the context of global digital economic integration, reliable and advanced cloud computing is playing an increasingly pivotal role in the logistics sector, especially in long-haul trunk logistics. The diverse characteristics of Logistics Information Systems, along with the necessity to handle substantial data volumes and adhere to stringent data protection regulations from several stakeholders, present considerable obstacles to information flow and sharing. This issue is particularly pronounced in China's logistics sector, which is predominantly comprised of small and medium-sized firms (SMEs). This study offers the Hyperconnected Trunk Logistics Alliance (HTLA) framework to tackle these difficulties by utilizing blockchain and big data technologies. The framework seeks to diminish obstacles between diverse systems employed by various stakeholders and promote the integration of Logistics Information Systems while safeguarding data privacy. The suggested data privacy solution ensures data confidentiality within the network and implements access control *via* smart contracts on a distributed ledger. The UILA platform is an innovative solution that fosters collaboration among stakeholders and elevates logistics service standards. The implementation of the "China National Logistics Hub Project" has shown significant efficacy in creating a reliable, cooperative, and transparent logistics network system, underscoring its potential for widespread application and practical utility.

Keywords: cloud computing, Hyperconnected Trunk Logistics Alliance, Logistics Information System, blockchain, big data

1. Introduction

Logistics Information Systems (LIS) are essential for improving logistics efficiency and guaranteeing superior service delivery, especially in trunk logistics. Traditional logistics operations are impeded by obstacles including information asymmetry and data confidentiality concerns among various nodes and stakeholders. A significant issue is the fragmentation and variability of Logistics Information Systems [1], which are frequently owned and administered by various independent businesses. The absence of integration hinders effortless information exchange while preserving data security. Furthermore, without a comprehensive big data platform, the storage, processing, and analysis of extensive logistical data pose considerable challenges, hindering the extraction of valuable business insights. Resolving these difficulties necessitates creative solutions that improve data interoperability, security, and analytical capabilities inside the logistics ecosystem.

Updating the Logistics Information System (LIS) [2] is imperative to address the changing requirements of the logistics sector, particularly concerning the standard nodes of the Project of China National Logistics Hub (PCNLH). This project is a comprehensive strategy aimed at improving the national logistics infrastructure, with hub nodes functioning as focal points for regional logistical operations. A promising paradigm that informs contemporary logistics systems is the Physical Internet (PI) [3]. PI seeks to integrate all components of logistics processes, encompassing hubs, containers, and participants, analogous to the manner in which the digital Internet interlinks information. This topic has garnered considerable interest from researchers and practitioners alike. A worldwide logistics system predicated on PI is engineered to integrate logistical networks *via* standardized cooperation protocols, modular containers, and intelligent interfaces. PI processes physical items in a manner akin to the handling of digital messages, borrowing inspiration from the digital Internet.

Protecting the security and privacy of logistics big data is a crucial issue. This problem is becoming more important, but current applications and technologies often fall short of safeguarding big data effectively. From a theoretical standpoint [4], Rubinstein analyzed how big data impacts privacy. A decentralized privacy method [5] was proposed to protect private data using a protocol and a blockchain as an automated access-control manager. Meanwhile, Li et al. [6] discussed the technical challenges of big data security and privacy, while Abdulsalam et al. [7] reviewed the key technologies for big data security. A secure big data storage method was introduced using compression and encryption [8]. More recently, blockchain technology, which powers Bitcoin, has been explored to address these issues [9]. Blockchain features hash algorithms, digital signatures, timestamps, consensus mechanisms, and smart contracts. It can verify data authenticity and protect privacy by anonymizing data providers and users. However, a recent smart contract scheme [10] still has limitations, such as failing to validate transaction signatures.

In summary, recent research shows that most studies lack a comprehensive solution for managing real big data in a big data environment. It remains a significant challenge to collect and use data while fully solving security and privacy issues.

This paper makes the following contributions:

First Cloud Computing Solution for China National Logistics Hub: We present a case study of applying cloud computing to the China National Logistics Hub project.

A novel logistics framework utilizing blockchain and big data: We present the Hyperconnected Trunk Logistics Alliance (HTLA) Computing Platform. This platform aims to integrate Logistics Information Systems (LISs) into a cohesive alliance.

Consolidated Application of Big Data with Blockchain: In HTLA, big data manages extensive and varied datasets, promoting collaboration among stakeholders. Blockchain enhances data confidentiality and optimizes service delivery.

The rest of this paper is organized as follows: Section 2 reviews related work, Section 3 introduces the components of the Hyperconnected Trunk Logistics

Alliance, Section 4 describes our approach, Section 5 presents a case study of the China National Logistics Hub project, and Section 6 concludes the paper.

2. Related work

2.1 Physical Internet

2.1.1 Physical Internet (PI)

The Physical Internet (PI) is envisioned as an open, globally integrated logistics network aimed at enhancing efficiency and sustainability throughout all logistical operations. It represents a transformation from conventional hub-and-spoke frameworks to dynamic, hyperconnected networks [11]. PI cultivates a highly collaborative logistics ecosystem by seamlessly combining physical components, like hubs and modular containers, with human and organizational participants. Inspired by the digital Internet, PI facilitates the standardized transfer of logistical data over many networks, adhering to standards similar to TCP/IP. This integrated architecture improves real-time communication, coordination, and resource sharing, thereby converting the logistics industry into a more flexible and robust system.

2.1.2 PI-container

Based on the concept of the Physical Internet (PI), products are encased in intelligent containers that are modularly engineered and easily interconnectable. These vessels, referred to as PI containers, are engineered for global compatibility. This indicates that any logistics provider may proficiently and autonomously manage, transport, and store products from any enterprise. Ref. [12] delineates three modular kinds of these containers, as depicted in **Figure 1**. Moreover, the author in Ref. [17] delineates the physical prerequisites for containers, outlining essential functional and physical characteristics.

The study [17] delineates the physical prerequisites for containers, outlining essential functional and physical characteristics.

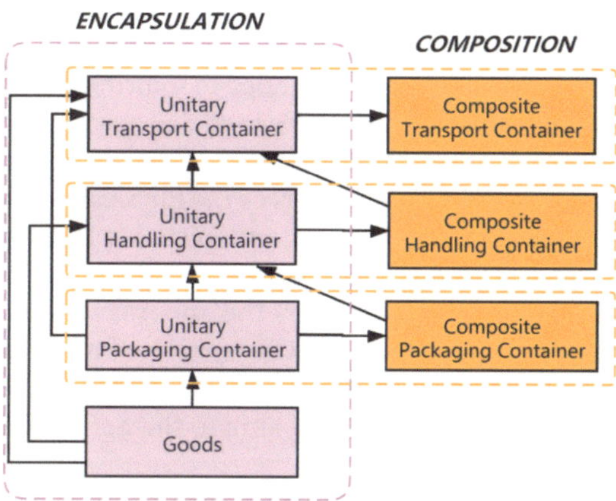

Figure 1.
The three categories of PI containers.

2.2 Blockchain applied in LIS

To develop and operate a big data platform for logistics systems, ensuring data authenticity and security is crucial. However, current big data management and security technologies are insufficient to fully meet these requirements. Consequently, robust privacy protection measures must be implemented to guarantee data integrity and authenticity.

Blockchain technology, with its inherent characteristics, appears to be a promising solution. However, its application and research in Logistics Information Systems (LIS) are still in their early stages. Some scholars have explored blockchain applications in logistics, traffic management, and transportation [13, 14], but these studies have yet to provide comprehensive solutions. For example, Fu and Zhu designed a consensus authentication mechanism and a smart contract to address risk management in certain supply chains [15]. Fan et al. proposed a model for sharing and exchanging government information resources [16]. Another study introduced an operational mechanism for Intelligent Logistics Systems based on blockchain [17], but it faced challenges related to efficient data storage and access speed due to blockchain's structural limitations.

Blockchain has been implemented in various supply chains, such as Wu Chain and Bubi Blockchain in China. Many of these blockchain systems differ from classical implementations like Bitcoin [9] and Ethereum [18, 19], highlighting the versatility of blockchain technology. Recently, a fully decentralized and confidential payment mechanism called Zether was proposed. It employs a novel smart contract to encrypt account balances and provides methods for depositing, transferring, and withdrawing funds while preserving user privacy.

In summary, while blockchain holds significant potential for addressing data security and privacy concerns, its application in logistics remains an evolving field. Further research and development are required to fully harness its capabilities.

3. Hyperconnected Trunk Logistics Alliance

3.1 Physical Internet enabled trunk logistics paradigm

3.1.1 Hyperconnected trunk logistics architecture

The hyperconnected logistics system is intended to improve the efficiency of products transportation *via* better package routing, accelerated delivery rates, and enhanced inventory management. We have developed an efficient framework for the trunk logistics system, incorporating the essential stakeholders of the Physical Internet (PI) network. This model consists of three consecutive layers, as depicted in **Figure 2**.

The proposed architecture markedly diverges from the traditional framework [20] and emphasizes the core network, specifically the upper layers, to simulate the trunk logistics network. It will introduce an innovative notion of a hub-access layer with standardized access requirements. This layer interacts with diverse local entities while reducing and generalizing their distinctions, akin to the network access layer in the TCP/IP framework.

In the organizational framework, many entities are identified as conventional Physical Internet (PI) organizations. These organizations utilize inter-organizational networks to facilitate collaborative and decentralized logistical operations, hence

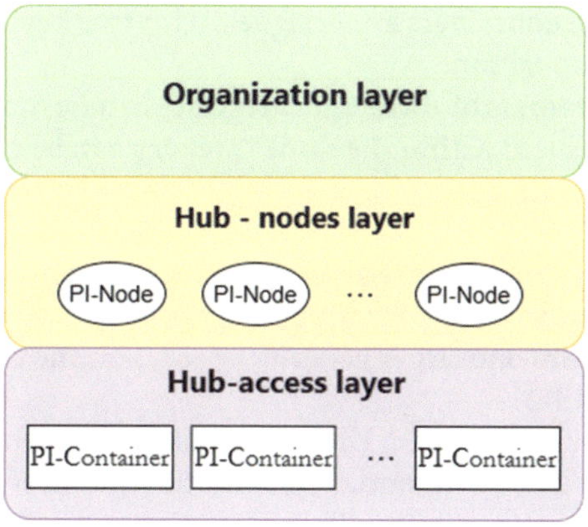

Figure 2.
Architecture of hyperconnected trunk logistics.

improving cooperation and cross-organizational efficiency. In this context, information flow can be optimally leveraged to oversee the network regulating the actual transportation of containers.

Furthermore, by incorporating blockchain and big data, we may create a groundbreaking Logistics Information System (LIS). This approach guarantees data confidentiality while augmenting the scientific rigor, logic, and intelligence of decision-making. Transportation routes can be organized in a more interconnected and flexible manner, instead of conforming to conventional point-to-point or hub-and-spoke arrangements. This method facilitates the dynamic and more efficient allocation of containers.

3.1.2 Hub in hub-nodes layer

PI nodes function as the primary hubs within the network [21], with logistics service providers (LSPs) being their essential components. Traditionally, logistics service providers function autonomously inside isolated logistical networks, constraining interoperability and collaboration. In the Physical Internet paradigm, a hub is characterized as a fully operational PI node—essentially a super node—within the truck logistics network. This hub fundamentally consists of an integrated logistics service provider (LSP), sometimes known as a super PI-LSP node. This entity is essential for optimizing logistics operations by overseeing crucial processes such as receiving, sorting, dispatching, and shipping, thereby improving overall efficiency and connection within the logistics framework.

3.1.3 Containers in the hub-access layer

In the hub-access layer, the basic unit of data exchange is associated with the container. These containers are intelligent, PI-based units known as PI containers. They can pack goods in a modular and standardized form. With the widespread use of these containers, any logistics service provider can conveniently and efficiently transport, exchange, and store products from any company.

To streamline the information flow in hyperconnected logistics networks, we enhance the PI-container concept from the work [12] in physical and informational aspects. Specifically, the containers are designed with two key relationships: Encapsulation and Composition.

Encapsulation: Containers of different categories can be nested within each other.

Composition: Containers within the same category can be combined and interlocked. This modular design allows for more effective and efficient handling and transportation.

As a result, logistics transactions can be conducted using containers and encapsulated forms. For example, a single transaction might involve one container (1:1), multiple containers within one larger container (N:1), or one container serving multiple transactions (1:N).

Each container is equipped with a Universal Unique Identifier (UUID) as its "identity card," and features data confidentiality, condition monitoring, compatibility, and interoperability, as well as traceability. These functions ensure the accurate transmission and management of logistics information.

Universal Unique Identifier (UUID): Each container has a unique "identity card" for identification and location within the logistics network.

Data confidentiality: Containers maintain a "black box" status to other participants, with access to loading/unloading or transportation data restricted to authorized participants only.

Condition monitoring: Participants can monitor the status data of goods inside the container (e.g., location and condition) in accordance with legal agreements.

Compatibility and interoperability: Containers can effectively communicate with the Logistics Information Systems (LIS) of different participants, even if these systems are heterogeneous.

Traceability and tracking: Containers can be located by LIS and provide traceable information, such as the actual status of goods, arrival and departure dates, and environmental conditions like temperature and humidity.

The users of the hub-access layer include shippers, consignees, hub nodes, transport service providers (TSPs), warehousing providers, and logistics service providers (LSPs). They play different roles in the logistics process and collectively drive the transportation and delivery of goods.

3.2 Hyperconnected Trunk Logistics Alliance model

This section introduces the Hyperconnected Trunk Logistics Alliance, a framework aiming to build a trustworthy, collaborative, and global logistics network as an alternative to closed systems. It also discusses Logistics Information Modules (LIMs) and the detailed structure of the alliance model supported by advanced technologies like blockchain and big data.

3.2.1 Hyperconnected Trunk Logistics Alliance

The Physical Internet (PI) concept has the potential to revolutionize business models by introducing a new paradigm of collaborative and decentralized logistics. This innovative approach is gaining increasing attention and practical application. Ideally, forming an alliance based on the PI concept, which includes all logistics entities such as producers, distributors, logistics service providers, transport service providers, and end-users, seems like an excellent solution. However, given the massive scale and complex requirements involved, this currently remains an ambitious goal.

Therefore, we propose a more pragmatic approach: an alliance of super hub nodes on the trunk logistics network, leveraging the PI concept. This alliance called the Hyperconnected Trunk Logistics Alliance (HTLA), can be easily implemented due to its streamlined structure.

In the HTLA, members are defined as integrated Logistics Service Providers (LSPs), typically modeled by nodes in the second layer of the hyperconnected trunk logistics architecture (as shown in **Figure 2**). The HTLA can provide global information services for interoperability and coordination, enabled by unified rules and protocols that each participating node must adhere to.

3.2.2 HTLA model based on blockchain and big data

The HTLA model is essentially based on blockchain and big data technologies, utilizing their capabilities to improve security, efficiency, and collaboration inside logistics networks. Blockchain addresses essential difficulties such as data confidentiality, real-time tracking and tracing of containers, automatic collaboration in decentralized settings, and the development of important information for supply chain finance. Furthermore, it guarantees that data contributors receive suitable compensation for their contributions.

Concurrently, big data functions as the foundation of effective logistical operations. It enables the amalgamation of disparate and fragmented Logistics Information Systems (LISs), improves system optimization *via* stakeholder participation, and aids regulatory supervision and policy formulation by governmental and industrial entities.

The HTLA model's architecture incorporates both distributed and centralized paradigms, as depicted in **Figure 3**. It functions as a distributed system similar to a standard consortium blockchain framework, enhanced by big data and cloud services to surpass conventional blockchain node capabilities. At the hub level, a centralized model is utilized, creating a cohesive platform that provides standardized services and interacts with stakeholders according to predetermined specifications. This hybrid methodology guarantees a cohesive, secure, and scalable logistics framework.

An essential advancement in our methodology is the creation of a new technique for segmenting and reconstituting container-related data. Containers are the essential units in logistics operations, rendering their associated data a vital resource due to their extensive utilization, as emphasized in the hub-access layer [23]. Nonetheless, disseminating this information across stakeholders poses considerable obstacles, chiefly due to apprehensions regarding data confidentiality stemming from competitive business dynamics and the necessity to safeguard economic interests.

To address these challenges, we have developed a solution that systematically processes container data. We specifically isolate critical private information—such as shipper and receiver details—from the general container data and manage it using specialized blockchain smart contracts. Residual non-sensitive data elements, without independent meaning, are put on a publicly accessible big data platform. This method promotes uninterrupted information services and allows for sophisticated big data analytics [24]. Moreover, utilizing the container's distinct UUID, these fragmented data elements can be safely reconstructed in diverse legal circumstances, facilitating capabilities such as real-time tracking and tracing for the recipient.

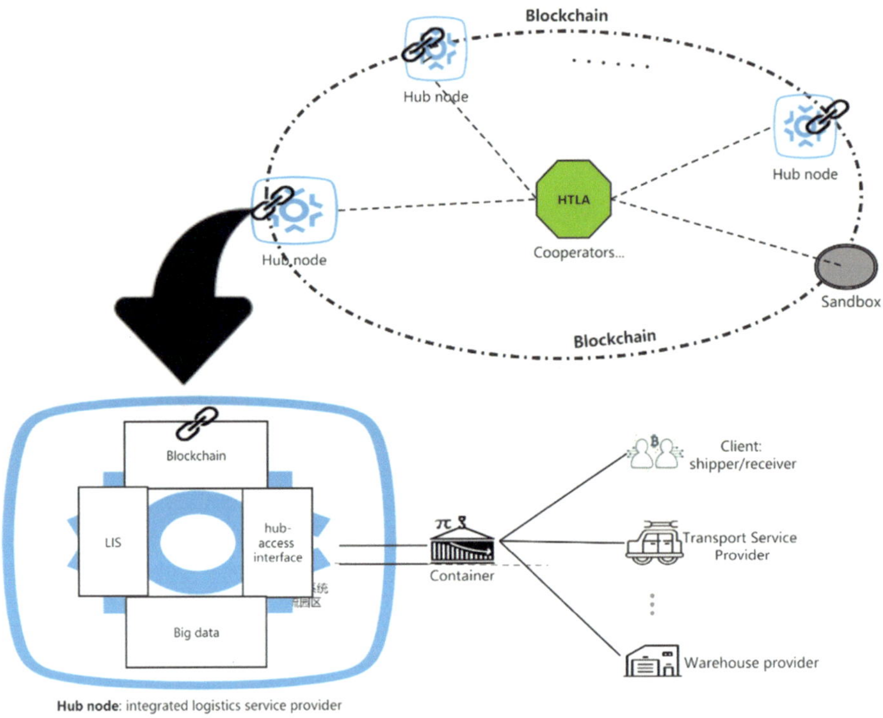

Figure 3.
The Hyperconnected Trunk Logistics Alliance (HTLA) based on blockchain and big data.

The suggested HTLA approach efficiently mitigates these limits by integrating blockchain and big data technologies, hence boosting the integrity and accessibility of logistical data. Blockchain guarantees data validity through stringent confidentiality management and access control procedures executed via smart contracts, thereby facilitating informed, data-driven decision-making. Concurrently, big data analytics enhances logistics operations by facilitating accurate analysis and informed decision-making, such as identifying the most efficient transit routes. This hybrid strategy not only fortifies data security but also improves operational efficiency throughout the logistics ecosystem.

4. Logistics Information System in the proposed HTLA model

Contemporary logistics necessitates the effective administration of multiple interrelated flows, encompassing products, vehicles, financial activities, and reverse logistics. Data and information flows are especially vital, as they facilitate the efficient management, coordination, and enhancement of all other logistical activities. Logistics operations encompass several stakeholders and organizations, utilizing Logistics Information Systems (LISs) to facilitate precise, safe, and efficient data exchange—frequently in real time.

Nonetheless, current Library and Information Systems (LISs) exhibit significant heterogeneity, producing enormous amounts of both organized and unstructured data. The real-time integration of these different systems presents considerable obstacles, mostly due to stakeholders' apprehensions regarding competitiveness, which obstructs data sharing and collaboration.

The HTLA concept presents a cohesive strategy for enhancing information service quality among alliance members *via* an advanced LIS platform. This platform is founded on two fundamental technological advancements:

Standardized cloud service: A cloud-based application and interface, created with a logistics big data platform driven by Hadoop and Spark, to augment data integration and boost interoperability among various LISs.

Blockchain for data confidentiality: guarantees data security, promotes trust among stakeholders, and alleviates hesitance to communicate information by protecting sensitive corporate data.

The HTLA model improves cooperation, optimizes logistics operations, and facilitates real-time, secure, and efficient data interchange throughout the logistics ecosystem by incorporating these technologies.

4.1 Big data

In contemporary Logistics Information Systems (LIS), big data is essential for enhancing logistics operations. Nonetheless, its vast volume, diversity, and variability pose considerable obstacles in data gathering, storage, and interpretation. This study presents a distributed big data platform, constructed on the Hadoop/Spark framework, to facilitate the hub nodes of the Hyperconnected Trunk Logistics Alliance (HTLA) in addressing these issues. This open-source system guarantees dependable, scalable, and distributed processing and analysis of extensive logistics information.

The data in HTLA hubs displays the essential attributes of big data—volume, diversity, velocity, and value—requiring a sophisticated infrastructure for effective handling. Subsystems producing smaller datasets can effortlessly join the platform using hub-access connections. This worldwide big data network, a crucial element of next-generation digital logistics, is interconnected across hubs through blockchain technology. The platform facilitates secure and regulated sharing of private data through the utilization of smart contracts and manual control measures, hence improving logistical efficiency, optimizing operational workflows, and promoting enhanced collaboration among stakeholders.

4.2 Blockchain

Establishing and overseeing a big data platform for logistics systems necessitates a robust data authenticity mechanism to guarantee security and reliability. Nonetheless, current big data security solutions are inadequate to completely fulfill these criteria, rendering the installation of enhanced privacy protection measures essential. Blockchain technology, characterized by decentralized consensus, data openness, auditability, and security feature, offers an ideal resolution to these difficulties.

This study presents a decentralized access control architecture utilizing blockchain to improve security and privacy in logistics data management. Access control is regulated using smart contracts, facilitating precise, efficient, and scalable permission management. Additionally, a cross-chain validation framework employing a two-way peg within a side blockchain enables cohesive access control across diverse logistics systems.

The HTLA model features a new access control framework that includes consensus authentication techniques, account privacy protection, and organized data access protocols. These components guarantee the security and secrecy of logistical, operational data while utilizing the inherent tracing attributes of blockchain. The

HTLA Computing Platform ultimately blends blockchain and big data technologies to facilitate seamless collaboration among stakeholders, successfully addressing data confidentiality issues and bolstering confidence within the logistics ecosystem.

5. Case study: A node of The Project of China National Logistics Hub

The significance of logistics is continually growing, especially due to heightened government backing. The Project of China National Logistics Hub (PCNLH) was formally unveiled in China on December 21, 2018. This strategic initiative involves the establishment of 127 logistical hubs, as seen in **Figure 4**, classified into six categories: 41 land-port hubs, 30 harbor hubs, 23 airport hubs, 47 production service hubs, 55 commerce service hubs, and 16 inland border hubs.

This case study examines a particular node inside the PCNLH, considering its distinct operating limitations, improving functions according to its hub categorization, and adjusting to the local business context. We specifically analyze the commerce service hub in Linyi, situated in the mid-eastern region of China. The principal problem resides in the intricacy of the local logistics ecosystem, which includes practically all types of logistics operations. This variability substantially elevates the functional requirements of the hub-access layer. The hub's principal function is to assist e-commerce suppliers by augmenting service capabilities, streamlining shipping processes, and promoting operational efficiency.

To address these problems, we devised a solution utilizing the proposed HTLA paradigm. The platform is organized as a distributed system, like a blockchain network, in which each alliance member operates as an autonomous blockchain

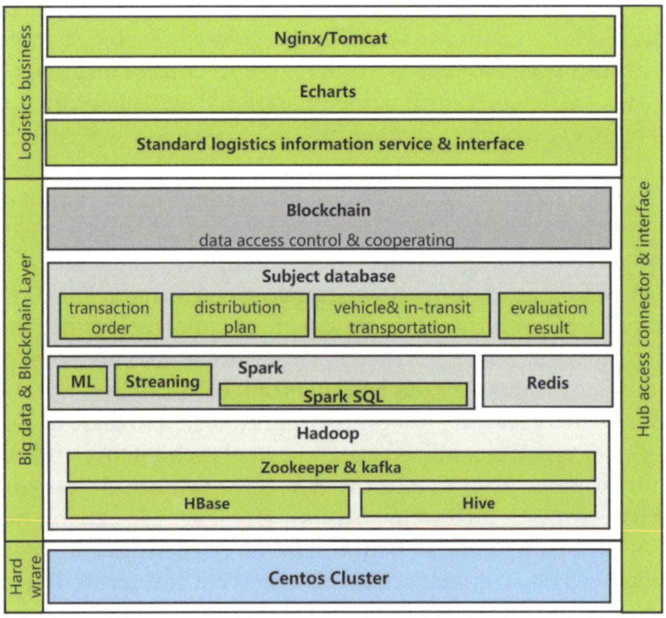

Figure 4.
A hub-node instance defined at the second layer in the HTLA Platform.

node. Additionally, each node is converted into a comprehensive Logistics Service Provider (LSP) platform, as illustrated in **Figure 4**. This platform consists of a localized large data center, a hub-access connector, containerized interfaces for efficient interaction with diverse logistics stakeholders, and a consolidated Logistics Information System (LIS) to standardize service provision. We meticulously chose suitable IT solutions to fulfill system requirements, utilizing the Hadoop/Spark framework for big data processing and incorporating Ethereum to create a safe and efficient blockchain architecture. This thorough strategy guarantees strong logistical operations, improved interoperability, and increased efficiency within the PCNLH framework.

These hub nodes act as blockchain nodes, forming a consortium blockchain platform. They store the full ledger and maintain the blockchain system by verifying and adding new blocks within the Ethereum framework. The underlying digital signature scheme uses ECDSA with the secp256k1 curve, and the hash algorithm employs SHA-256. Smart contracts play a crucial role in facilitating private data exchange and enabling cooperation in a legally compliant manner.

Leveraging the functionalities and characteristics of blockchain, this innovative computing paradigm addresses the challenges of sharing and exchanging sensitive data, particularly among competitors. Data ownership and control are retained by the data owner, ensuring security and eliminating the need for third-party intervention. Additionally, the decentralized nature of the blockchain system supports simpler legal and regulatory frameworks for collecting and sharing private data. Meanwhile, big data ensures standardized data sources, moving away from heterogeneity. The hub-access connector and interface establish a unified data-sharing standard with various socio-economic stakeholders. In turn, the unified Logistics Information System (LIS) service naturally aligns with this data standard.

6. Sustainability development significance

The research findings strongly align with the Sustainable Development Goals (SDGs) through the introduction of the Hyperconnected Trunk Logistics Alliance (HTLA) framework. The HTLA framework utilizes blockchain and big data technologies to improve logistics efficiency and decrease logistics costs relative to Gross Domestic Product (GDP), therefore promoting economic sustainability. The framework enhances equitable and competitive market conditions by facilitating smooth coordination among stakeholders and augmenting transparency within the logistics network. Moreover, blockchain technology guarantees strong data security and privacy, protecting the rights and interests of consumers and enterprises alike. The HTLA framework is especially advantageous for markets dominated by small and medium-sized enterprises (SMEs), such as China's logistics sector, by supplying the necessary technology foundation for growth and advancement. This, consequently, promotes inclusive economic growth. The HTLA framework is essential for sustainability as it optimizes logistics routes, minimizes superfluous traffic, and mitigates carbon emissions and environmental damage. Moreover, by stimulating technical innovation and knowledge sharing, the framework encourages overall societal advancement and supports long-term sustainable development. HTLA functions as a transformative solution for establishing a more efficient, equitable, and environmentally sustainable logistics ecosystem through its diverse contributions.

7. Conclusion

This study presents a unique logistics cloud computing framework, the Hyperconnected Trunk Logistics Alliance (HTLA), and illustrates its applicability *via* a case study. The HTLA framework offers a novel solution to critical logistical difficulties, such as information asymmetry, data confidentiality, and the integration of various logistical Information Systems (LISs) among different nodes and stakeholders, in comparison to current methods. The HTLA framework enhances digital transformation and operational efficiency in the logistics industry by adeptly addressing the difficulties of large-scale and diverse logistics environments. HTLA nodes, directly linked to the alliance's offline members, facilitate seamless collaboration and interoperability. Each node operates as a self-sufficient entity, furnished with a substantial data center and a cloud service platform. This design improves logistics performance and substantially decreases logistics costs relative to Gross Domestic Product (GDP), utilizing modern blockchain and big data technologies. To assess the practical consequences of this approach, we executed a case study centered on a node from the Project of China National Logistics Hub (PCNLH). We expect that the next research will investigate the scalability and adaptability of the HTLA framework in international logistics and cross-border trade, hence enhancing its influence on the global logistics environment.

Acknowledgements

This work was supported by the Taishan Industrial Experts Program (tscy20221187) and Shandong Provincial Natural Science Foundation (No. ZR2022MF331).

Author details

Deqian Fu*, Yaxian Jing, Ziqi Liu, Zhanling Shi, Zanmei Wu, Jinze Ma and Qianhui Ma
School of Information Science and Technology, Linyi University,
Linyi City, Shandong Province, China

*Address all correspondence to: fudeqian@lyu.edu.cn

References

[1] Yu X, Li P, Li SF. Research on data exchange between heterogeneous data in logistics information system. In: 2010 2nd International Conference on Communication Systems, Networks and Applications. Vol. 1. ICCSNA; 2010. pp. 127-130

[2] Grover N, Shaikh SJ, Faugère L, et al. Surfing the Physical Internet with hyperconnected logistics networks. In: 9th International Physical Internet Conference. Athens, Greece; 2023

[3] Münch C, Wehrle M, Kuhn T, Hartmann E. The research landscape around the physical internet—A bibliometric analysis. International Journal of Production Research. 2023;**62**(6):2015-2033

[4] Rubinstein IS. Big data: The end of privacy or a new beginning? International Data Privacy Law. 2013;**3**:74

[5] Yang D, Ye B, Zhang W, et al. KLPPS: A k-anonymous location privacy protection scheme via dummies and stackelberg game. Security and Communication Networks. 2021;**2021**(1):9635411

[6] Li H, Wang Y, Guo F, et al. Differential privacy location protection method based on the Markov model. Wireless Communications and Mobile Computing. 2021;**2021**(1):4696455

[7] Abdulsalam YS, Hedabou M. Security and privacy in cloud computing: technical review. Future Internet. 2021;**14**(1):11

[8] Lv D, Zhu S, Liu R. Research on big data security storage based on compressed sensing. IEEE Access. 2019;7:3810-3825

[9] Xia T, Zhang W, Chiu WS, et al. Using cloud computing integrated architecture to improve delivery committed rate in smart manufacturing. Enterprise Information Systems. 2021;**15**(9):1260-1279

[10] Betti Q, Khoury R, Hallé S, et al. Improving hyperconnected logistics with blockchains and smart contracts. IT Professional. 2019;**21**(4):25-32

[11] Fu D, Hu S, Zhang L, et al. An intelligent cloud computing of trunk logistics alliance based on blockchain and big data. The Journal of Supercomputing. 2021;**77**(12):13863-13878

[12] Sallez Y, Pan S, Montreuil B, Berger T, Ballot E. On the activeness of intelligent Physical Internet containers. Computers in Industry. 2016;**81**:96-104

[13] Tijan E, Aksentijević S, Ivanić K, Jardas M. Blockchain technology implementation in logistics. Sustainability. 2019;**11**(4):1185-1187

[14] Tian YS, Zhao GH, Shen LY. Block chain transportation: Taking freight logistics and the market governance as the example. China Business and Market. 2018;**32**(2):50-56

[15] Fu Y, Zhu J. Big production enterprise supply chain endogenous risk management based on blockchain. IEEE Access. 2019;7:15310-15319

[16] Fan J, Zhang P, Yen D C. G2G information sharing among government agencies. Information & Management. 2014;**51**(1):120-128

[17] Fu Y, Zhu J. Operation mechanisms for intelligent logistics system: A blockchain perspective. IEEE Access. 2019;7:144202-144213

[18] Buterin V. Ethereum White Paper. 2014. Available from: https://github.com/ethereum/wiki/wiki/White-Paper

[19] Wood G. Ethereum: Yellow Paper. 2016. Available from: http://gavwood.com/paper.pdf

[20] Bünz B, Agrawal S, Zamani M, et al. Zether: Towards privacy in a smart contract world. International Conference on Financial Cryptography and Data Security. Cham: Springer International Publishing; 2020. pp. 423-443

[21] Li H, Guo F, Wang L, et al. A blockchain-based public auditing protocol with self-certified public keys for cloud data. Security and Communication Networks. 2021;**2021**(1):6623639

[22] Stefanovic N. Big data analytics in supply chain management. Encyclopedia of Organizational Knowledge, Administration, and Technology. IGI Global Scientific Publishing. 2021:2443-2457

[23] Song W, Zhang W, Zhai L, et al. EOS. IO blockchain data analysis. The Journal of Supercomputing. 2022:1-32

[24] Peng C, Liu Z, Wen F, et al. Research on blockchain technology and media industry applications in the context of big data. Wireless Communications and Mobile Computing. 2022;**2022**(1):3038436

Chapter 4

Orchestrating Data Center Bring-Up: Efficient Strategies for Scalable Infrastructure Deployment

Dmitry Shchemelinin, Andrei Kazakin and Andrei Marchenko

Abstract

This chapter presents the design and implementation of a comprehensive data center orchestration framework optimized for Artificial Intelligence (AI)-centric workloads. The proposed approach explores the complexities of automating large-scale infrastructure bring-up across the world, with a focus on overcoming challenges specific to regional deployments, including hardware heterogeneity, network configuration, and resource allocation. The proposed solution integrates scalable automation workflows and monitoring mechanisms to ensure consistency, reliability, and operational efficiency across deployments. By adopting a structured orchestration methodology, the proposed framework facilitates reduced time-to-service, improved fault tolerance, and enhanced scalability, making it well-suited for dynamic, high-performance computing (HPC) environments typical of modern AI applications.

Keywords: deployment automation, infrastructure orchestration, infrastructure as a code, hardware bring-up, operational efficiency

1. Introduction

In the digital age, modern technology companies depend on robust, scalable, and reliable data center infrastructure to power their global services. The complexity of managing large-scale server deployments is a critical challenge that requires sophisticated strategies, precise planning and coordination, and advanced operational techniques. The ability to efficiently deploy, manage, and scale server hardware is no longer just an operational requirement - it's a competitive advantage that can define an organization's technological capabilities.

This chapter explores the methodologies and strategies that enable organizations to orchestrate large-scale data center operations while maintaining the resilience necessary for today's demanding digital landscape.

The focus of this research centers on an enterprise-level cloud platform which provides advanced infrastructure for developers and researchers with a comprehensive environment for testing, optimizing, and deploying complex applications and algorithmic solutions. The platform offers a variety of virtual machines (VM), bare-metal (BM) systems, edge devices, and platforms designed for AI training [1].

Deploying and managing such a complex, geographically distributed cloud platform demands sophisticated tooling and advanced automation strategies. The infrastructure relies on comprehensive automation frameworks that enable:

- Consistent infrastructure provisioning across regions
- Automated configuration management
- Seamless network and security policy enforcement
- Resource allocation and scaling
- Rapid deployment and reproducibility of computing environment.

Automation is not merely a convenience but a fundamental requirement for managing such a complex, multi-regional computing ecosystem. Each deployment requires precise orchestration of:

- Infrastructure as Code (IaC) principles
- Continuous integration and deployment
- Advanced monitoring and observability tools.

Setting up a private data center in a new geographic region is a complex technical challenge. The infrastructure includes many interconnected systems and coordinating them requires a high degree of automation. By automating deployment and management processes, organizations can reduce the risk of human errors, improve consistency, and ensure smoother integration across all components.

The architectural blueprint of a modern data center is organized into several distinct layers, each with a specific set of responsibilities for computing and networking.

1. Network services foundation layer: An advanced networking architecture is the core of a datacenter [2]. A sophisticated network fabric that provides high-bandwidth interconnects, low-latency communication pathways, intelligent routing and traffic management, and software-defined networking (SDN) capabilities. This layer also includes core network services such as Domain Name System (DNS), Dynamic Host Configuration Protocol (DHCP), and load balancer solutions, and provides automated resource assignment and granular management capabilities, laying the groundwork for the entire data center's operational ecosystem.

2. Bare-metal layer: The bare-metal layer consists of physical servers and specialized hardware. This layer delivers essential compute, networking, and storage functionalities, serving as the foundational infrastructure of the data center

3. Virtualization layer: On top of the bare-metal infrastructure, virtual machines are deployed within kernel-based virtual machine (KVM) clusters [3]. This vir-

tualization layer abstracts physical resources, enabling flexible, software-defined environments. It promotes better maintainability and optimizes the utilization of computing resources by decoupling workloads from the underlying hardware.

4. Containerization and orchestration layer: The next layer introduces container technologies and orchestration platforms. Kubernetes clusters are deployed here to manage both stateless and stateful workloads efficiently [4]. This layer underpins microservices architectures and automates tasks such as load balancing, service discovery, scaling, and failover, greatly simplifying operations through powerful orchestration capabilities.

5. Storage solutions: A dedicated storage layer is incorporated to provide reliable, scalable and high-performing data management for both customer-facing services and internal operations.

6. Additional appliances: Depending on the specific requirements of the data center, additional software and hardware appliances may be integrated at various layers. These appliances enhance security, accelerate performance, or provide specialized services tailored to application and business needs.

Deploying resources in a private cloud requires careful planning and execution, and the use of reliable tools. Commonly used solutions include Ansible [5] for configuration management, Jenkins [6] for automation, and Ironic for provisioning bare-metal servers [7]. Depending on the resource type, teams might need multiple detailed configuration playbooks to effectively set up and manage each component.

To provide a more comprehensive view it is important to add the following conditions:

- Distributed team ownership: Multiple specialized teams manage discrete components, creating a decentralized operational model.

- Evolving architecture: The private cloud's architecture is a continuously evolving framework, adapting to emerging technological paradigms and organizational requirements.

- Regional customization: Each geographical area demands distinct customizations to accommodate local infrastructure capabilities and operational differences. These adaptations are also driven by specific product requirements and the unique needs of customers in each region.

- Global collaboration: Teams distributed across distant time zones operate in a 24/7 model to efficiently bring up the data center. This continuous collaboration approach requires robust mechanisms for transferring deployment state, sharing contextual knowledge, and ensuring operational continuity across shifts. Clear documentation, automated status updates, and well-defined handover processes are critical to avoid duplication of effort, reduce downtime, and accelerate delivery.

Each deployment step serves as a critical prerequisite for the next phase. In practice, however, infrastructure components are often delivered in a less-than-ideal state, leading to extended periods of troubleshooting and root cause analysis. At first glance, manual deployment may seem appealing due to the sense of direct control it offers. Teams might feel empowered by their ability to make immediate adjustments, believing that a hands-on approach provides maximum flexibility and precision. However, as deployment complexity grows the weaknesses of manual methods start to show:

- Manual errors: Increased risk of misconfigurations and inconsistencies
- State tracking: Lack of clear deployment status complicates handoffs between teams working across time zones
- Process repetition issues: Difficult to ensure consistency across regions
- Error reproducibility: Hard to identify and debug failures.

Through multiple regional deployments, we realized that true operational excellence goes beyond just deployment. It demands a comprehensive approach that redefines how we design, implement, and manage infrastructure. We identified the need for a robust orchestration solution, which is described in detail in this document. This solution enables us to:

- Maintain an accurate and actual state of managed resources
- Improve transparency and auditability of operations
- Minimize manual errors
- Provide extension points for validation and codified operational knowledge
- Manage dependencies between resources efficiently.

Figure 1 illustrates the evolution from a manually managed system – where engineers directly trigger and maintain multiple Ansible and Jenkins jobs – to an orchestrated model. On the left, individual management of jobs shows a significant

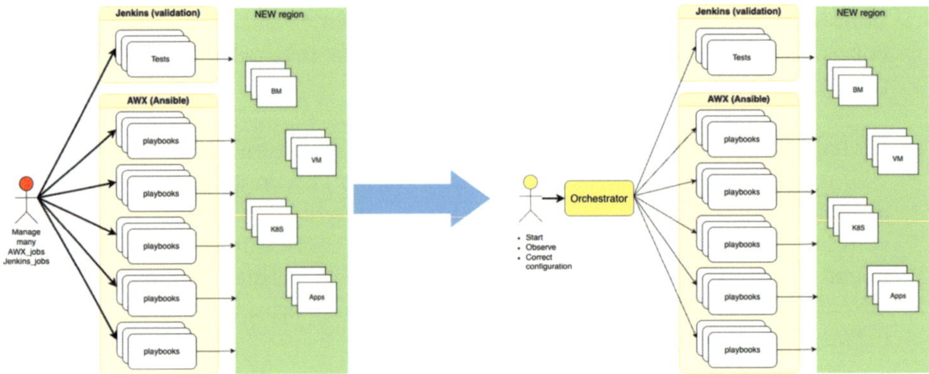

Figure 1.
Operational transformation.

operational overhead. On the right, the new solution introduces an Orchestrator that centralizes execution and coordination. This automation layer eliminates the need for manual coordination of individual jobs, reduces operational complexity, and allows engineers to focus more effectively on higher-value engineering tasks.

2. Principles of implementation

At the heart of the solution is a desire to make the process of bringing up a new region as autonomous as possible. Several principles were employed to achieve this:

- Codified knowledge: It includes (as a critical component) automatic tests to validate and accept infrastructure. AI-assisted development greatly simplifies this task.
- Idempotence of operations.
- Declarative high-level building blocks while at the same time we can retain low-level procedural tasks.
- Explicit dependencies between resources.
- Set of holistic resources (defined by properties with schema/types) forms an application programming interface (API). This approach is preferable to proliferation of variables.
- Controller pattern compares desired declarative state with the actual state and allows to specify actions to eliminate the difference.

2.1 Codified knowledge

Standard and proven by time best practices comprising software development lifecycle (SDLC) are applicable for infrastructure code as well.

Properly defined objective, documented requirements and succinctly defined design enables controlled implementation. Such an approach allows several people to contribute to the same solution whether they collocated in the same office or spanned over different time zones.

Testing plays a pivotal role and needs to be automated as well. As shown in [8] emulation with Linux virtual machines allows to validate network topology, servers, firewalls, and so on, using minimal resources and development effort. For example [9], shows usage of Ansible for automated connection test as the productive approach.

The recent work [10] on building a cloud infrastructure for virtual machines scheduling showed the effective usage of Ansible [5] (in conjunction with Zabbix [11]) as IaC solution.

2.2 Idempotence of operations

The rise of cloud computing and large dynamically scaling distributed applications brought to existence configuration management tools which should provide robust and repeatable software deployment processes.

Many configuration management tools (one of the most famous initial solutions is CFEngine© [12], see also [13]) operate on a declarative description which represents different resources concerning the desired system state.

The resource actions can fail temporarily but are expected to eventually succeed. In other words, the system should converge to the desired state. Once the system is successfully installed and matches the desired configuration, the tool should be able to reapply the same actions without causing unintended changes. As shown in the work [14] the crucial prerequisite for the convergence is execution of idempotent actions.

Researchers build rigorous models to attest reliable convergence (one of the most prominent examples is [15]) or make it part of criteria assessing overall quality [16].

2.3 Declarative high-level building blocks

As noted in [17] most infrastructure languages are declarative languages rather than imperative ones. Such an approach is useful for defining the desired state of a system and it is common to define the repeatable and consistent shape of infrastructure.

However, sometimes there is a need to write code that can produce different outcomes depending on the situation. As declarative code supports more complex variations, it involves increasing amounts of logic.

And when declarative code is infused with increasing amounts of orchestration it can quickly become unsupportable. The presented solution offloads orchestration logic into separate entity.

Also, it is worth noting that at the lowest level it is ok to use imperative code. The system should be flexible enough to support both styles of infrastructure code.

2.4 Explicit dependencies between resources

Managing large collections of infrastructure resources provisioned for cloud platform requires special tooling. For example, in [17] such class of software is called stack management tools. Typical representatives are Terraform [18] and CloudFormation [19]. CloudFormation is a solution specific for Amazon Web Services (AWS) cloud and Terraform do not provide all capabilities. But both tools provide critical property for building stacks—management of dependencies between resources and ordering of operations for them.

2.5 Flexible resource-oriented approach

Various configuration management tools have their own approach toward configuration. The classic way for the configuration as a code is to rely on variables as the simplest concept.

However, such an approach can quickly become unmanageable. For example, in the case of Ansible there are 22 levels of precedence [20] which is much more complicated compared to many widespread general programming languages.

For example, Terraform introduced domain specific language (DSL) called HashiCorp Configuration Language (HCL) where focus is on resources and their properties. The language allows us to describe inter-connections between properties of various resources reducing this way usage of variables and enhancing graph of dependencies.

Another example is Declarative application management in Kubernetes [21]. The approach is based on observations of several dozen configuration projects and hundreds of configured applications within Google [22] and in the Kubernetes ecosystem, as well as quantitative analysis of Borg configurations and work on the Kubernetes.

2.6 Controller pattern

In robotics and automation, a control loop is a non-terminating loop that regulates the state of a system. In cloud environments the idea of control loops has been popularized by Kubernetes [23]. Controllers are control loops that watch the state of a cluster and request changes where is needed. Each controller tries to move the current cluster state closer to the desired state.

As a tenet of its design, Kubernetes uses lots of controllers that each manage a particular aspect of cluster state. It is important design principle to prefer simple controllers rather than one, monolithic set of control loops that are interlinked. Controllers can fail, so Kubernetes is designed to allow for that.

Controller pattern is an essential part not only Kubernetes but the whole approach toward management of infrastructure resources. There is a term which recently has been coined in the industry - "Configuration as Data" (see [24]). Even Terraform community adopted this approach in the form of "HCP Terraform Operator for Kubernetes" [25] and "Tofu Controller" [26].

This pattern brings a new level of autonomy.

3. Considered alternatives

The solution presented in this chapter is not a theoretical research prototype, but rather a practical implementation selected and adopted within an enterprise environment. Consequently, it is essential to contextualize the decision-making process and discuss the various options that were evaluated.

3.1 Option 1: Increasing complexity within Ansible

Our initial implementation was built on Ansible, leveraging its simplicity and strong community support. Given limited resources and the desire for rapid delivery, we explored the possibility of remaining within the Ansible ecosystem.

While Ansible is a powerful orchestration tool, its yet another markup language (YAML) based configuration language is not general-purpose and imposes constraints on expressing complex logic. Our goal was to maintain a clean separation of concerns and avoid embedding orchestration logic too deeply into infrastructure definitions.

Although using tools like AWX [27] (an open-source project maintained by Red Hat® as the upstream of Red Hat Ansible® Automation Platform) to structure playbooks into workflows can be effective for provisioning a single bare-metal device, this approach becomes fragile at scale. A key limitation is the inability of AWX to resume execution mid-process after a failure—a concern highlighted in issue [28], where users from large organizations express a need for resilient, long-running workflows. In our own experience, deployment cycles can span multiple days, depending on environmental readiness.

In summary, overloading Ansible with orchestration responsibilities leads to brittle, monolithic workflows—prompting us to investigate more modular and resilient solutions.

3.2 Option 2: Apache airflow

The workflow orchestration landscape is vast, and Apache Airflow stands out as a mature, production-grade system. According to a comparative analysis of Workflow Management Systems (WMS) [29], Airflow is a leading task-driven platform and is widely adopted across industries.

However, several factors made Airflow suboptimal for our specific use case:

- Airflow's design is centered around *task orchestration*, not *resource management*. In contrast, modern infrastructure tooling prioritizes resource state and lifecycle.

- It was originally designed to support large-scale batch processing, making it less aligned with infrastructure deployment needs.

- Its user interface allows for rich introspection and manual intervention. But infrastructure engineers expect managed resources as long-living entities with their own life cycle (served by autonomous, tested procedures).

Given these limitations, we concluded that Airflow was not the most suitable choice for our orchestration layer.

3.3 Option 3: Terraform

Terraform is a cornerstone in the IaC ecosystem. It is extensible, widely adopted, and excels in public cloud environments. However, when applied to private data centers and custom resource types, Terraform reveals notable gaps:

- It does not provide autonomous execution or self-healing capabilities out-of-the-box.

- Its strength lies in declarative provisioning, but it requires significant custom development when working outside its native provider ecosystem.

Given that substantial code investment was needed regardless of platform, we questioned whether Terraform was the optimal target for such custom extensions. This led us to explore more natively extensible solutions.

3.4 Option 4: Kubernetes operators

Kubernetes has become a foundational platform not only for container orchestration but also for building extensible, API-driven infrastructure systems. Several factors contributed to our decision to adopt Kubernetes Operators as the orchestration layer:

- Mature ecosystem of tooling, libraries, and deployment frameworks.

- Availability of skilled practitioners and a strong community.

- Established best practices, security standards, and high availability models.
- Native support for custom resources and controller/operator patterns, making it ideal for modeling infrastructure as code.

The broader industry trend of configuration as data further validated our direction. Major cloud providers have embraced Kubernetes-native orchestration:

- AWS Controllers for Kubernetes (ACK) [30] for Amazon Web Services
- Azure Service Operator (ASO) [31] for Microsoft Azure
- Config Connector [32] for Google Cloud Platform
- Crossplane [33], a cloud-agnostic, extensible control plane for custom resource management.

In addition, the vibrant ecosystem of operator development frameworks in multiple languages ensures flexibility and long-term maintainability. In this context, we use the terms controller and operator interchangeably, both referring to software agents that manage the lifecycle of custom Kubernetes resources.

4. Architecture

A core component of the orchestration solution is a set of Kubernetes controllers that manage custom resources within a cluster (**Figure 2**). These *custom resources* serve as declarative representations of the deployment state and act as coordination points for dependent processes. Their current state is transparent to engineers, enabling operational insight and automation. Leveraging the *controller pattern*—which inherently includes reconciliation loops and retry mechanisms—ensures a resilient, autonomous bring-up process. This autonomy allows engineers to prioritize high-value activities such as resolving complex issues, cross-team collaboration, and overseeing semi-manual integration steps.

Controllers and their associated custom resources must reside within a Kubernetes cluster. Depending on organizational constraints and project requirements, this control cluster can be deployed in either a public or private cloud. In the reference architecture (**Figure 2**), the orchestration layer is encapsulated within a logical unit labeled as the *Management Account*. This environment requires minimal but secure network connectivity to the new data center region being provisioned.

4.1 Management account

The Management Account houses the orchestration control plane and supporting tools. As depicted in **Figure 2**, it typically includes components familiar to the DevOps community:

- AWX, serving as an execution engine for Ansible playbooks
- Jenkins, providing general-purpose automation and job orchestration.

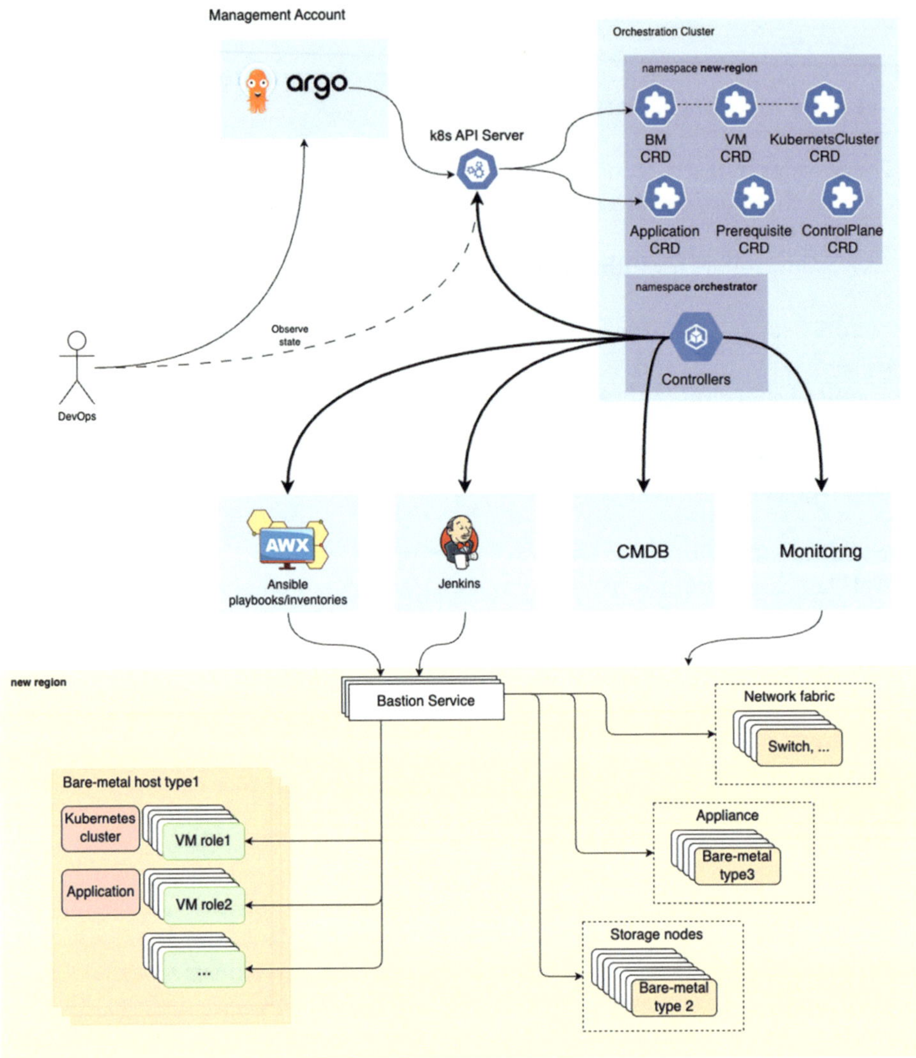

Figure 2.
Architectural diagram.

These tools can be substituted with alternatives aligned to an organization's preferences or cloud-native stack. For example, one might adopt Kubernetes-native CI/CD tools or other frameworks based on team expertise and system requirements.

Two other notable components are the configuration management database (CMDB) and Monitoring system:

- For CMDB, open-source solutions such as NetBox can serve as a centralized source of truth for infrastructure metadata.

- Monitoring tooling is more organization-specific and may include Prometheus, Grafana, or commercial platforms depending on observability needs.

Additionally, ArgoCD plays a pivotal role in enabling GitOps-driven deployments into Kubernetes clusters. The orchestration controller interfaces with ArgoCD and the

Kubernetes API to guide and monitor the deployment lifecycle across target environments. Further detail on workflow integration is provided in Section 5.

4.2 New region deployment

Bringing up a new region involves the coordinated construction and configuration of a complex network fabric. In our implementation, communication with the new site is routed through a dedicated bastion service, making it one of the first components to be provisioned. Once base connectivity is established, bare-metal servers are initialized to host foundational services and virtual machines.

A local Kubernetes cluster acts as a universal control plane, providing a consistent and extensible environment for deploying essential platform services. In real-world scenarios, multiple independent Kubernetes clusters—each with specialized roles—are deployed to support diverse workloads. These clusters often come with distinct networking, storage, and policy requirements.

All components must be architected with high availability (HA), performance, and scalability in mind, ensuring that the new region meets enterprise-grade reliability and operational standards from day one.

5. Workflow and change management

Security, safety, and process governance must be addressed from the earliest stages of system design. We start it with the following question: What roles exist in the deployment process, and how can we ensure changes are implemented safely and correctly?

To address this, our orchestration system is built upon GitOps principles—a model that combines declarative infrastructure management with version-controlled change approval processes. This methodology supports auditable, secure, and reproducible deployments, and has been explored in recent literature [34, 35].

In our implementation, GitOps is operationalized through ArgoCD, which acts as the reconciliation agent between version-controlled configuration and the target Kubernetes clusters [36].

5.1 Deployment sequence

Figure 3 illustrates the general sequence of operations when bringing up a new region:

1. Namespace preparation: A designated *Administrator* provisions a Kubernetes namespace specific to the new region. This creates a bounded context and limits the scope of resource operations.

2. Configuration submission and review: A *DevOps engineer* prepares a set of declarative resource manifests (e.g., YAML files) and submits them via a pull request (PR) to a Git repository. While GitHub is commonly used, any version control system supporting PR reviews and audit trails is acceptable. The PR undergoes mandatory peer review by designated process owners before it can be merged, ensuring compliance, accuracy, and security.

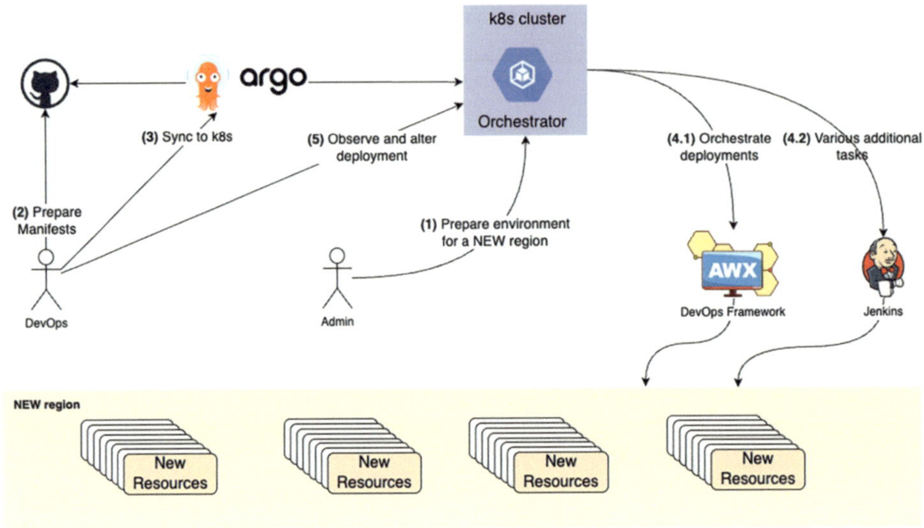

Figure 3.
Deployment sequence.

3. Resource synchronization: Upon approval and merge into the main branch, ArgoCD initiates synchronization of the manifests with the appropriate cluster and namespace. This ensures that the actual system state reflects the desired configuration defined in Git.

4. Workflow orchestration: Once the target state is reconciled in the cluster, the orchestration controller triggers execution of dependent workflows—such as Ansible playbooks in AWX or automation tasks in Jenkins—according to defined custom resources and control logic.

5. State monitoring and interventions: Engineers can monitor the deployment progress using standard Kubernetes tools such as kubectl or k9s. If intervention is needed, predefined behaviors can be triggered by annotating custom resources, allowing for controlled modifications without disrupting the declarative model.

This workflow ensures traceability, consistency, and minimal manual intervention while preserving flexibility for controlled operational overrides. By combining GitOps practices with Kubernetes-native tooling, the system maintains a balance between automation and human oversight.

6. State management

As previously discussed, each custom resource reflects a segment of the deployment process and maintains a structured state. This state is fundamental for coordinating orchestration workflows and is best conceptualized as a composition of interconnected state machines (**Figure 4**).

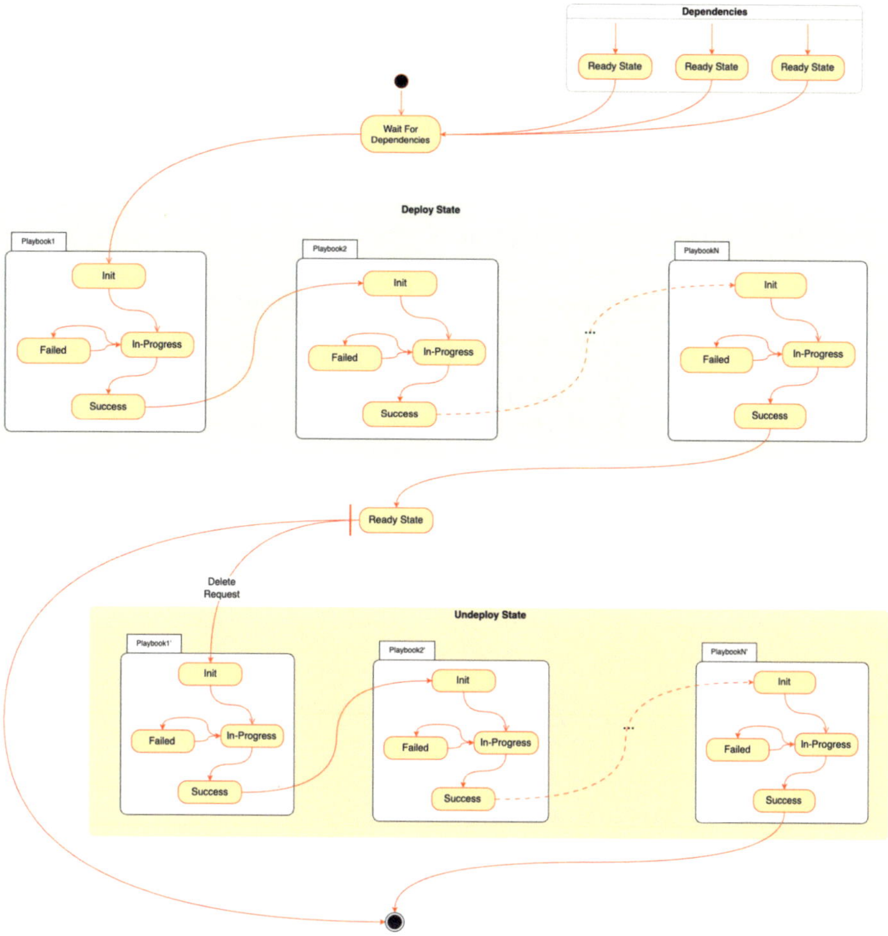

Figure 4.
State diagram.

6.1 Readiness state and dependency graph

At the most basic level, every resource possesses a readiness state, typically represented as a binary flag (Ready or not). A resource marked as ready signifies that its deployment has been successfully fulfilled and downstream operations may proceed.

These relationships form a dependency graph, which encodes the orchestration logic. Traversing this graph enables the orchestrator to evaluate whether a given resource is eligible for deployment or whether it must defer execution until prerequisite resources reach a valid state. This enhances transparency and control over complex bring-up sequences.

6.2 Plan execution state

To achieve its target state, each resource is associated with a deployment plan, which comprises an ordered sequence of tasks. The plan state captures:

- The identifier or name of the active plan
- The specific task currently being executed.

This plan-based abstraction provides fine-grained control over execution progress and supports partial retries or resumption strategies.

6.3 Task state and external integration

At the lowest level, individual tasks within the plan are executed, potentially via external systems. The task state varies depending on the execution method:

- For example, in our current implementation, this may include an AWX Job ID or a Jenkins Job ID, linking the task to an external process.
- At a minimum, task progress is tracked using a simple status enumeration such as: Init, In-Progress, Failed, Success.

If a task fails and cannot automatically recover (e.g., due to external dependency failure or unexpected system conditions), detailed diagnostics must be exposed to the engineering team for manual intervention and remediation.

This layered state model—spanning readiness, plan execution, and task lifecycle—enables modular, observable, and robust orchestration of infrastructure deployments.

7. Operator configuration and custom resources

The orchestration system is centered around Kubernetes custom resources (CRs), which encode desired deployment states. These CRs are interpreted and acted upon by

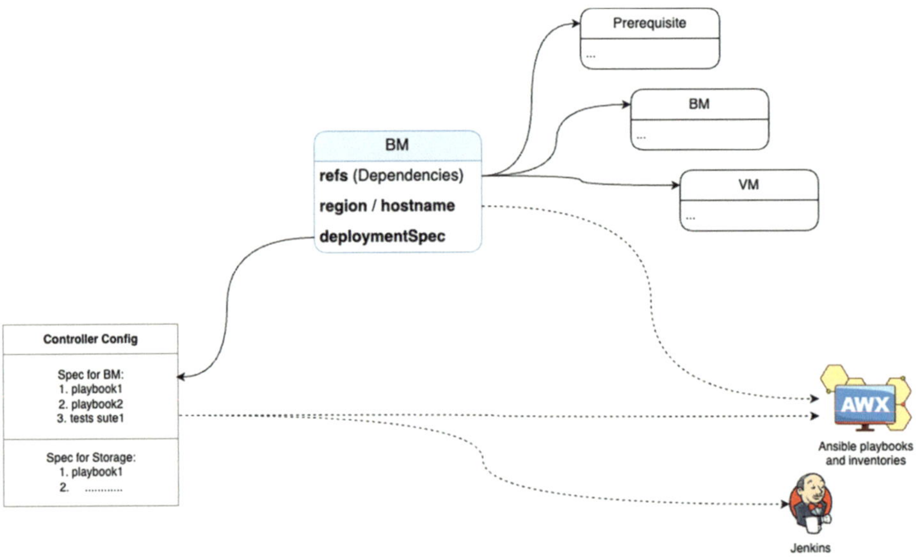

Figure 5.
Resource, configuration, and external systems diagram.

specialized controllers (operators), enabling declarative, event-driven management of infrastructure components. See **Figure 5** for a visualization of the interconnection between the resource specification, operator configuration, and external systems.

7.1 Custom resources

The orchestration framework supports the following custom resource types:

- Prerequisite
- BM
- VM
- Application
- KubernetesCluster
- ControlPlane.

These CRs are intentionally defined with minimal specifications, sufficient to support three primary goals:

- Reference to automation systems: Each resource can identify itself in AWX and Jenkins, ensuring traceability to provisioning logic.
- Dependency definition: Resources can describe their relationships to other resources, enabling orchestration through a dependency graph.
- Scenario mapping: Each resource references a deployment scenario, defined in the operator configuration, which dictates the steps required to transition the resource to a ready state.

The status section of each CR captures real-time operational information, including readiness, failure reasons, and execution identifiers. This allows DevOps engineers to quickly assess the progress and health of the deployment.

7.2 Operator configuration

To reconcile the desired state expressed in each resource, the operator requires configuration that defines how to interact with external systems and contextualize the deployment environment. Key aspects of the operator configuration include:

- External system mappings:
    - Kubernetes namespaces: Logical scopes for deployment, typically isolated by region or environment.
    - AWX inventories: Host groups and target machines relevant to each deployment region.
    - Jenkins configuration items: Pipeline jobs, credentials, or parameter sets linked to specific resources.

- Scenario definitions:
    - o Declarative specifications that describe how each type of resource is deployed, including task sequences and orchestration boundaries.

The configuration must be flexible and extensible, supporting the creation of new regions and roles without requiring code changes in the operator itself. This separation of control logic (in the operator) and deployment semantics (in configuration) enhances modularity, reuse, and adaptability.

8. Conclusions

The adoption of a robust orchestration solution significantly transformed the way infrastructure is deployed and managed across our private cloud environments. By introducing a consistent, codified approach to resource provisioning, configuration, and lifecycle management, we observed improvements in key operational metrics:

- Faster deployment times: Infrastructure deployment timelines were reduced from 1 to 2 weeks to just 1–2 days. This acceleration in deployment speed represents a fundamental shift in our ability to respond to business needs.

- Fewer human errors: The orchestrator provides centralized and unified logging capabilities that enable tracking of misconfigurations, environmental inconsistencies, and remediation activities. We have implemented continuous measurement, monitoring, and comparison of error frequencies across deployments, providing valuable insights into system reliability and areas for ongoing improvement.

- Improved operational transparency: Custom Resource Definitions in Kubernetes provide real-time status tracking of complex deployment processes. The core advantage is in establishing a single source of truth, eliminating configuration drift. This approach also improves debugging capabilities and embeds operational knowledge into the declarative specification.

- Enhanced consistency across regions: The orchestrator manages custom resources uniformly, ensuring that the same application specifications and operational parameters are consistently applied across all regional resources. This standardization reduces the environment-specific variations

- Simplified support and maintenance: Operations teams have a convenient single pane of glass for managing infrastructure across all environments and regions. Reduced context switching eases the mental load of working with different systems and methods across regions. Support engineers use the same interfaces, commands, and workflows throughout the global infrastructure

Implementing the orchestration framework has drastically improved our overall time to market, transforming what was once a lengthy, sequential process into a rapid, parallel deployment model.

Acknowledgements

This work is supported by and implemented at Intel Corporation, CA, USA [1].

Author details

Dmitry Shchemelinin*, Andrei Kazakin and Andrei Marchenko
Intel Corporation, Santa-Clara, CA, USA

*Address all correspondence to: dshchmel@gmail.com

References

[1] Intel® cloud products official website [Internet]. 2025. Available from: https://www.intel.com/content/www/us/en/developer/tools/tiber/ai-cloud.html [Accessed: May 5, 2025]

[2] Gao Z, Zheng X, Wang Z. Design of the data center network architecture under the background of cloud computing: A review. World Journal of Innovative Management & Technology (WJIMT). 2024;**3**(2):55-61. DOI: 10.53469/wjimt.2024.07(04).07

[3] Gandhi U, Modi M, Raval M, Maniar P, Patel N, Sharma K. Distributed virtualization manager for KVM based cluster. Procedia Computer Science. 2016;**79**:182-189. DOI: 10.1016/j.procs.2016.03.024

[4] Al Jawarneh IM, Bellavista P, Bosi F, Foschini L, Martuscelli G, Montanari R, et al. Container orchestration engines: A thorough functional and performance comparison. In: Proceedings of the 2019 IEEE International Conference on Communications (ICC). Los Alamitos, USA: IEEE; 2019. pp. 1-6. DOI: 10.1109/ICC.2019.8762053

[5] Hochstein L, Moser R. Ansible: Up and Running. 2nd ed. Sebastopol, USA: O'Reilly Media; 2017. 430 p. ISBN-10: 1491979801, ISBN-13: 978-1491979808

[6] Laster B. Jenkins 2: Up and Running. 1st ed. Sebastopol, USA: O'Reilly Media; 2018. 604 p. ISBN-10: 1491979593, ISBN-13: 978-1491979594

[7] Ironic ® bare metal as a service [Internet]. 2025. Available from: https://ironicbaremetal.org [Accessed: May 5, 2025]

[8] Craiu G, Catrina O. Fast prototyping and testing of network security solutions using virtualization and Ansible. In: 2024 15th International Conference on Communications, COMM 2024. Los Alamitos, CA, USA: IEEE; 2024

[9] Haruta A, Masuda H, Yamaoka H, Akiyama T, Yamamoto K, Tamai K, et al. An attempt of on-demand automated connection test suite for updating network infrastructure. In: 50th ACM SIGUCCS User Services Annual Conference, SIGUCCS, Chicago. New York, NY, US: Association for Computing Machinery (ACM); 2023. pp. 29-31

[10] Chua J, Jiang X. Building a cloud infrastructure for virtual machine scheduling in datacenters. In: 2024 IEEE 14th Annual Computing and Communication Workshop and Conference, CCWC. Los Alamitos, USA: IEEE; 2024. pp. 105-110

[11] Olups R. Zabbix Network Monitoring. 2nd ed. Grosvenor House, Birmingham: Packt Publishing; 2016. 754 p. DOI: 10.5555/3074244

[12] Burgess M. Site configuration engine. Computing Systems. 1995;**8**(3):309-337

[13] Burgess M, Couch A. Modeling next generation configuration management tools. In: LISA 2006 - 20th Large Installation System Administration Conference. Berkeley, CA, United States: USENIX Association; 2006. pp. 131-147

[14] Couch A, Sun Y. On the algebraic structure of convergence. Lecture Notes in Computer Science (including subseries Lecture Notes in Artificial Intelligence and Lecture Notes in Bioinformatics). 2003;**2867**:28-40

[15] Hanappi O, Hummer W, Dustdar S. Asserting reliable convergence for

configuration management scripts. In: Proceedings of the Conference on Object-Oriented Programming Systems, Languages, and Applications, OOPSLA, 02-04-November-2016. New York, NY, US: Association for Computing Machinery; 2016. pp. 328-343

[16] Kumara I, Garriga M, Romeu AU, Di Nucci D, Palomba F, Tamburri DA, et al. The do's and don'ts of infrastructure code: A systematic gray literature review. Information and Software Technology. 2021;**137**:106593. DOI: 10.1016/j.infsof.2021.106593

[17] Morris K. Infrastructure as Code. 3rd ed. Sebastopol, CA, USA: O'Reilly Media, Inc; 2025. 436 p. ISBN-10: 109815035X; ISBN-13: 978-1098150358

[18] Brikman Y. Terraform: Up and Running: Writing Infrastructure as Code. 3rd ed. Sebastopol, CA, USA: O'Reilly Media, Inc; 2022. 457 p. ISBN-10: 1098116747, ISBN-13: 978-1098116743

[19] Tovmasyan K, Mastering AWS. CloudFormation: Plan, Develop, and Deploy your Cloud Infrastructure Effectively Using AWS CloudFormation. 1st ed. Birmingham: Packt Publishing; 2020. 300 p. ISBN-10: 178913093X, ISBN-13: 978-1789130935

[20] Understanding variable precedence [Internet]. 2025. Available from: https://docs.ansible.com/ansible/latest/playbook_guide/playbooks_variables.html#understanding-variable-precedence [Accessed: May 7, 2025]

[21] Declarative application management in Kubernetes [Internet]. 2025. Available from: https://github.com/kubernetes/design-proposals-archive/blob/main/architecture/declarative-application-management.md [Accessed: May 7, 2025]

[22] Burns B, Grant B, Oppenheimer D, Brewer E, Wilkes J. Borg, omega, and Kubernetes: Lessons learned from three container-management systems over a decade. ACM Queue. 2016;**14**(1):70-93. DOI: 10.1145/2898442.2898444

[23] Official Kubernetes website [Internet]. 2025. Available from: https://kubernetes.io [Accessed: May 8, 2025]

[24] Configuration as data [Internet]. 2025. Available from: https://cloud.google.com/blog/products/containers-kubernetes/understanding-configuration-as-data-in-kubernetes [Accessed: May 8, 2025]

[25] HCP terraform operator for Kubernetes [Internet]. 2025. Available from: https://developer.hashicorp.com/terraform/cloud-docs/integrations/kubernetes [Accessed: May 8, 2025]

[26] Tofu controller [Internet]. 2025. Available from: https://github.com/flux-iac/tofu-controller [Accessed: May 8, 2025]

[27] Sullivan S. Demystifying Ansible Automation Platform: A Definitive Way to Manage Ansible Automation Platform and Ansible Tower. Birmingham: Packt Publishing; 2022. 314 p. ISBN-10: 1803244887; ISBN-13: 978-1803244884

[28] Feature idea: Resume workflow from point of failure. Issue 1284 [Internet]. 2018. Available from: https://github.com/ansible/awx/issues/1284 [Accessed: May 8, 2025]

[29] Mitchell R, Pottier L, Jacobs S, Silva RFD, Rynge M, Vahi K, et al. Exploration of workflow management systems emerging features from users perspectives. In: Proceedings - 2019 IEEE International Conference on Big Data, Big Data 2019, Art. no. 9005494. Los Alamitos, CA, USA: IEEE; 2019. pp. 4537-4544. DOI: 10.1109/BigData47090.2019.9005494

[30] Controllers for Kubernetes (ACK) [Internet]. 2025. Available from: https://aws-controllers-k8s.github.io/community/docs/community/overview/ [Accessed: May 8, 2025]

[31] Azure service operator v2 [Internet]. 2025. Available from: https://azure.github.io/azure-service-operator/ [Accessed: May 8, 2025]

[32] Config connector [Internet]. 2025. Available from: https://cloud.google.com/config-connector/docs/overview [Accessed: May 8, 2025]

[33] Crossplane [Internet]. 2025. Available from: https://www.crossplane.io/ [Accessed: May 8, 2025]

[34] Limoncelli TA. GitOps: A path to more self-service IT. Queue. 2018;**16**(3):13-26. DOI: 10.1145/3236386.3237207

[35] Beetz F, Harrer S. GitOps: The evolution of DevOps? IEEE Software. 2022;**39**(4):70-75. DOI: 10.1109/MS.2021.3119106

[36] Ramadoni UE, Fatta HA. Analysis on the use of declarative and pull-based deployment models on GitOps using Argo CD. In: ICOIACT 2021 - 4th International Conference on Information and Communications Technology: The Role of AI in Health and Social Revolution in Turbulence Era. Los Alamitos, CA, USA: IEEE; 2021. pp. 186-191. DOI: 10.1109/ICOIACT53268.2021.9563984

Chapter 5

Exploring the Impact of AI-Driven Cybersecurity Frameworks on Data Privacy, Security, and Resource Optimization in Cloud Environments

Waleed Almuseelem

Abstract

Cloud computing has gained traction in the last decade, with many organizations migrating their computing infrastructure to the cloud. Cloud technology provides various benefits to both cloud providers and customers. The migration of computing infrastructure from on-premises to the cloud has helped organizations avoid complexities and challenges associated with non-virtualized computing infrastructure. Cloud computing helps organizations lower operational costs associated with on-premises infrastructure such as energy and physical security. Cloud providers offer low costs regarding access and usage of computing infrastructure as various businesses share computing resources. However, the main challenge of moving computing infrastructure to the cloud is the robust need for cybersecurity. AI and ML have proven to be effective solutions to the ever-evolving cloud security landscape. This chapter used Hands-on, where Amazon Macie from AWS was used to automate the threat detection and response. The results demonstrated that Amazon Macie helped enhance cloud security and privacy and optimized computing resource usage.

Keywords: cloud computing, data security, data storage, cybersecurity, potential threats, resource optimization, artificial intelligence, machine learning, energy-efficient, AI-driven

1. Introduction

The introduction of cloud computing has revolutionized how organizations perform their operations in terms of data storage, processing, and management [1]. Cloud computing refers to a model system that enables the on-demand delivery of computing resources via the Internet. Migration of computing infrastructure into the cloud has enabled organizations to save on operational costs such as energy that would have powered on-premises computing infrastructures. However, migration of computing infrastructure to the cloud presents security and privacy challenges as cloud environments are vulnerable to cyber threats and unauthorized access via the internet. Additionally, cyber threats are ever-evolving, presenting the challenge for traditional security mechanisms to catch up. In this regard, cloud security has become a vital aspect of cloud environments, presenting the need to ensure the integrity and confidentiality of cloud environments.

According to Olabanji et al. [2], AI and ML have proven to be significant in adapting to the ever-evolving cyber threats, becoming a vital factor for cloud security. Oduri and Sailesh [3] state AI, from a cybersecurity perspective, entails tools that can analyze big datasets, identify patterns, predict threats, and respond to threats in real time. The predictivity capability of AI is based on patterns identified from historical data on attacks and threats to cloud security. The integration of AI models into cloud cybersecurity allows the automation of defense mechanisms.

The rise of AI and ML has seen cyber threats utilize the technology to perform attacks, gain unauthorized access, and perform malicious acts with breached sensitive information. The usage of AI models in cyber threats allows the automation of attacks, presenting the need to establish advanced security mechanisms with integrated AI models to detect anomalies and act accordingly. Additionally, the cloud computing landscape is ever-evolving, presenting the need to use scalable security mechanisms such as AI-driven cybersecurity frameworks. The scalability nature of AI systems enables the utilization of security measures that adapt to real-time changes.

According to Harris and Lorenzaj [4], AI is pivotal to sustainable cloud computing. AI cybersecurity frameworks offer innovative solutions that enhance efficiency and sustainability within cloud environments. Harris and Lorenzaj [4] state that the International Energy Agency (IEA) report showed data centers accounted for approximately 1% of global electricity demand in 2020. Cloud energy consumption is rising due to many organizations' increased cloud adoption. Many energy sources used to power the various data centers rely on fossil fuels, negatively impacting the environment. AI technologies in cloud environments are equipped with machine learning algorithms that can optimize resource allocation, reducing the energy consumption of cloud infrastructure.

However, integrating AI into cloud cybersecurity comes with challenges. Relying on AI systems that analyze a vast amount of cloud data introduces privacy and data integrity risks. Cloud providers are responsible for ensuring that cybersecurity frameworks' AI operations operate with unbiased data and respect user privacy, complicating the required algorithm designs.

This chapter explores how AI-driven cybersecurity Frameworks impact Data Privacy, Security, and Resource Optimization in Cloud Environments. The literature highlights the status of AI technologies present in cloud security today. The current problems and challenges of AI-driven cybersecurity practices are reviewed to highlight how AI technologies are reshaping the security of cloud-based systems. The researcher also proposes a solution to help address the identified problems and challenges of AI-driven cybersecurity. The researcher also uses the AWS cloud platform to simulate the proposed solution to help examine how AI-driven solutions impact privacy and security and contribute to sustainable development via optimized resource utilization. The simulation results based on the automation of threat detection and response to risks present an AI-driven cybersecurity framework that ensures safety and resilient cloud environments.

2. Literature review

2.1 AI technologies in cybersecurity

Various studies have deeply explored the implementation of AI in cybersecurity, focusing on how security protocols are enhanced via ML, anomaly detection, and pattern recognition [3]. Nama and Prathyusha [5] described AI as the ability of a system to work on data, learn, and make decisions. The decisions are made using algorithms drawn from available data based on mathematical models. AI systems based on big data can provide meaningful insights, improving operational efficiency and the overall user experience of cloud environments.

The scalability nature of cloud environments has enabled AI models to use adequate computing resources necessary for training the AI models. The combination of AI and cloud computing has enabled the following powerful applications and services: Analytics solutions where a vast amount of cloud data is analyzed to extract meaningful insights. Cloud providers such as AWS use analytics solutions to optimize operations. AI algorithms can identify patterns and trends from analyzed datasets to help organizations make data-driven decisions to improve their operations. The patterns and trends identified help AI algorithms improve security via continuous monitoring for suspicious activities, enabling anomaly detection and response to threats in real time. Threat detection and response are responsible for automating security practices and reducing the risks of cyber-attacks. Additionally, AI is powered to adjust computing resources dynamically, enabling optimization of resource use that helps reduce costs by avoiding the underutilization of resources [5]. Muppa and Kaushik Reddy [6] showcased the dynamic capabilities of AI in adapting security architectures to use computing resources to protect cloud environments effectively. Muppa and Kaushik Reddy [6] also highlighted the predictive capabilities of AI in identifying potential security threats, enabling defensive responses to threats that can cause harm, and improving the overall security mechanisms of cloud environments. The studies highlighted the importance of AI in improving threat detection and automating response capabilities, making cloud environments more efficient.

2.2 Current integrations of AI in cloud security

The reviewed literature highlighted several studies that focus on AI integration in cloud environments. For instance, Abdullahi et al. [7] aimed to examine the integration of AI-based security measures to improve the security of the Internet of Things (IoT). The study findings showed that AI models are effective in safeguarding IoT. Another study by Aldridge et al. [8] explored how AI may be utilized to analyze corporate fillings and generate reports. The study showed that AI can help organizations improve accountability and governance. Aruna et al. [9] explored AI from the aspect of software development. The study concluded that AI is significant in ensuring resilient and secure software solutions as it is equipped with features that reduce software security vulnerabilities. Gundu et al. [10] focused on how AI integration can help reduce mobile cloud security risks. The results demonstrated that AI was key in safeguarding sensitive data in transit or at rest in mobile networks. Ismatullaev et al. [11] focused on the implications of AI systems integration on user behavior. The study concluded that AI systems affect consumers' acceptance based on privacy risks.

2.3 AI-driven strategies for resource efficiency

According to Harris and Lorenzaj [4], organizations can use AI's predictive analytics to focus their computing resource quantity required for smooth operations. Predictive analytics rely on ML to make surge predictions and adjust accordingly. Harris and Lorenzaj [4] state that Google's AI system reduced its data centers' energy consumption for cooling systems by 40%. Google's AI system scenario highlighted that AI can be used to allocate resources optimally, reducing energy wastage.

The automation of AI systems in cloud environments helped eliminate various manual steps of a cloud computing process, minimizing energy consumption and thus promoting sustainability. AI systems also improve operational efficiency as they eliminate human errors that lead to the usage of more resources. Therefore, AI systems optimize resource utilization via automation, promoting sustainability in cloud environments.

3. Problems and challenges

3.1 Overview of cloud security challenges

Cloud computing has become popular due to its benefits, such as flexibility, cost reduction, and scalability of its computing infrastructure, unlike the situation of on-premises computing infrastructures. However, migration of computing infrastructure to the cloud, such as data storage, introduces security and privacy risks regarding unauthorized access to sensitive information via cyber-attacks. Cloud computing's demand increase makes cloud platforms an ever-evolving landscape. In this regard, cyber threats based on unauthorized access are ever-evolving as well.

According to Mamidi [1], cloud environments need advanced security mechanisms that can adapt to the ever-evolving cyber threats. The recent rise of AI and ML has become vital in providing innovative cloud security solutions. AI and ML models can analyze big datasets and identify patterns. Pattern identification helps AI models report current threats as well as predict threats. The adaptability of AI models via ML has made the technology key to improving cloud security.

Understanding the various cyber threats is crucial for cyber experts to establish innovative solutions. According to Mamidi [1], understanding the evolving landscape of cyber threats is significant in identifying AI and ML algorithms that adapt to the threats. The following are some of the evolving cyber threats.

Data breaches via unauthorized access affect the confidentiality and integrity of cloud data. Unauthorized access to sensitive information may make organizations vulnerable to ransom attacks. Ransomware attacks normally target sensitive information or crucial systems and prevent authorized users from accessing their information or services. Sensitive data may be encrypted via a ransom attack. The attacker only releases the decryption key when a ransom is paid or a condition of a certain condition is met. Organizations under ransom attacks normally experience financial losses associated with downtime regarding business operations and ransom payments to avoid data loss. The theft of personal and financial data via ransom attacks or data breaches has become a lucrative business for cybercriminals.

Organizations are also vulnerable to Distributed Denial of Service (DDoS) attacks when they migrate their data to the cloud. DDoS attacks infiltrate a flood of traffic to a network or a system, rendering the computing resource inaccessible to legitimate users. Cloud computing involves interconnected network devices, making cloud environments vulnerable to DDOS attacks, as the attacks may target one or more cloud infrastructures to render them inaccessible.

Despite the financial loss in terms of interruption of business operations and costs to restore services to normalcy, organizations that have experienced cyber-attacks have damaged their reputation [1]. Successful cyber threats erode trust among stakeholders, customers, and partners. Rebuilding the reputation comes at a cost and is time-consuming.

The introduction of the IoT due to the advancement of cloud computing has enabled the operation of devices remotely. IoT relies on the internet to operate the services remotely, creating entry points for cybercriminals to interrupt device operations. Suppose one system of interconnected systems is breached, and the other systems become vulnerable, impacting the entire network's security. Addressing attacks in interconnected systems is complex as security professionals find it challenging to find cyber threats at entry points in vast connected systems [1].

3.2 Technical challenges of AI-driven cloud security

Integrating AI into cloud environments can be technically complex [1]. Compatibility is one of the main issues, as organizations need to ensure that their systems can handle the requirements of AI algorithms. AI models require continuous monitoring of computing resources for anomaly detection and reporting of threats in real time. The continuous monitoring requirement of AI models may require intense computing resources, straining available resources. Technical challenges may disrupt normal operations and the vital security of cloud environments. There is a need for careful planning regarding when to integrate AI systems so that the downtime of services and operations has minimal impact [12].

The complexity of AI algorithms requires a large quantity of computing resources, increasing computational costs during AI integration and implementation. Despite the running cost of used processing resources, the data used to train AI models require vast storage, introducing storage costs for organizations. Cloud part forms may increase the cost of their AI models since they consume vast amounts of energy as well. Organizations need to consider AI models that use fewer resources, promoting sustainability via effective resource use [12].

3.3 Data quality and availability

The integration of AI models into cloud environments introduces privacy risks based on the confidentiality of data used to train the AI models. Training of AI models requires big datasets retrieved from users, presenting the issue of how their data is used and the type of individuals who access the data. AI models may make decisions on their own and provide a response to a threat. Users may fail to understand how AI models make decisions, presenting the challenge of transparency. Additionally, users may find it difficult to assess the potential privacy risks of the AI models.

The type of data used to train the AI models has an impact on AI outcomes. AI models trained on low-quality data may make poor decisions, which negatively impact responses regarding defensive measures. Relying on high-quality data helps avoid biased outcomes for AI models [12].

AI training may target data from certain populations or criteria to make decisions, presenting discriminatory issues. Data used to train AI may be compromised via data breaches, compromising the integrity of the outcomes. AI models may also make inaccurate decisions due to false information injected by cybercriminals via cyber-attacks [12].

3.4 Skill gap challenge

According to Sudheer and Anoop [12], AI training and integration require a skilled workforce, which may not be present in many organizations. Skill gaps make organizations hire new skilled staff or train the existing workforce to equip them with AI skills. In this regard, the organization may incur additional costs due to the training and hiring of new staff. For smooth operations, organizations are required to have a skilled workforce to provide AI-driven solutions.

4. Proposed solution

The rise of cloud computing has led many organizations to adapt the technology to help reduce operational costs as well as take advantage of the flexibility and scalability nature of cloud environments [1]. Cloud technology eliminated the need for organizations to rely on many complex operations regarding on-premises resource utilization. However, the increase in cloud adoption presents various security vulnerabilities that cybercriminals may target.

According to Mamidi [1], AI and ML model integration in cloud platforms has become vital [1]. AI models rely on ML algorithms to analyze data and make threat predictions via pattern recognition and pattern matching. AI and ML can learn from historical data based on analyzed big datasets. The analysis of historical data is crucial for anomaly detection. AI systems can be configured to make alerts when threats are detected or predicted based on historical data analysis. ML identifies vulnerability by learning from previous threats. AI systems can perform automated defense, enabling real-time response to security and privacy threats.

However, combining AI with cloud computing presents challenges such as legal and ethical requirements, data quality, skills gap, and technical complexity, which are discussed in the above “Problems and Challenges” section. Additionally, AI models consume vast amounts of energy, impacting the environment as many energy sources still rely on fossil fuels. The researcher considered an AI model from AWS known as Amazon Macie to simulate the implementation of an AI-driven cybersecurity framework to identify its impact on data privacy, security, and resource optimization.

According to AWS [13], Amazon Macie is an AWS data security service that can identify sensitive data via ML and pattern matching, provide insights into data security risks, and allow automated protection against identified risks. The proposed solution will rely on Amazon Macie to automate threat detection and alerts to trigger incident response. The researcher will create an Amazon S3 bucket and a storage unit and upload sensitive data. The researcher will also configure Amazon Macie to continuously evaluate the created Amazon S3 bucket for anomaly detection of issues such as unencrypted buckets. Amazon Macie also automatically evaluates and monitors buckets and provides a policy finding if an issue regarding security or privacy is detected.

According to AWS [13], analyzing vast amounts of data to detect sensitive information can incur high costs due to the intense computing operations involved. Amazon Macie has various features that help businesses or organizations reduce costs while discovering sensitive data. The researcher aims to use Amazon data discovery, a custom-built feature for Amazon S3, equipped with new data sampling techniques to reduce costs. Additionally, automation of data discovery, as Macie’s feature is enabled by default, minimizes the quantity of data scanning in the Amazon S3 bucket, optimizing resource usage. These Macie features that assist with cost reduction rely on energy optimization algorithms that significantly reduce energy consumption in Amazon's data center. Reducing the quantity of computing resources used directly reduces energy used to power the computing resources, promoting the Sustainable Development Goals (SDGs).

5. Experiments in real cloud

This chapter utilizes a hands-on approach to examine the performance of AI-driven cybersecurity frameworks about data privacy, data security, and resource optimization. AWS platform implemented the AI-driven cybersecurity framework focusing on Amazon Macie. Macie provides estimated usage costs to help users manage their costs. Additionally, Macie offers a free trial, during which there is no charge for using Macie to evaluate and monitor storage units and stored data. The free trial may include automated sensitive data discovery, which complies with regulations such as GDPR. After the free trial ends, Macie provides users with estimated usage costs based on their usage during the trial period. Macie was used to analyze data stored in Amazon S3, a managed cloud storage solution that stores data as objects in a bucket. When a user enables Macie, it automatically creates a service-linked role that allows it to call other services and monitor computing resources on its behalf. Objects uploaded to the bucket entail AWS login credentials, which are sensitive information. The following are the steps of how Amazon Macie was configured.

5.1 Hands-on

An AWS demo account was utilized to create and test the service and examine Amazon Macie's effectiveness regarding cloud security, privacy, and resource optimization.

5.1.1 Step 1

The first step was to set up permissions for a user to access the Amazon Macie console and API operations. The IAM dashboard was used to set up the user, as shown in **Figure 1**.

Figure 1.
IAM user creation.

5.1.2 Step 2

AWS IAM was used to attach the AWS-managed policy AmazonMacieFullAccess to the user, as shown in **Figure 2**.

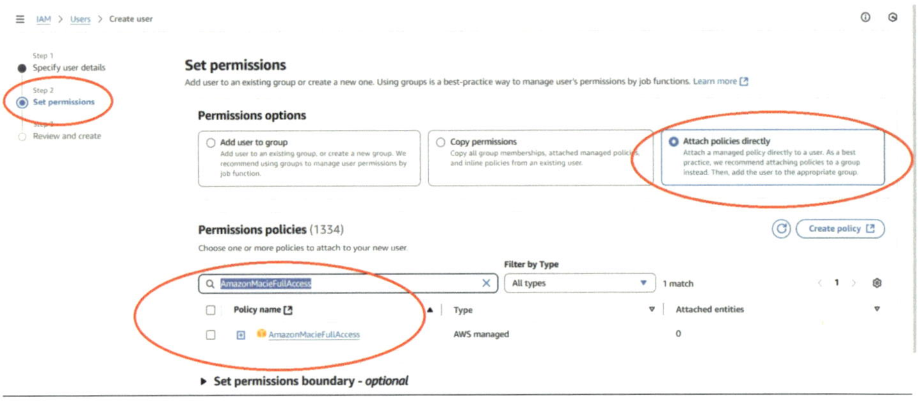

Figure 2.
Set up of permissions.

5.1.3 Step 3

The next step after setting up users and permissions is creating an Amazon S3 bucket. Amazon S3 is a managed cloud storage solution that helps users store data as objects in buckets, which are logical containers for objects. The Amazon S3 dashboard was used to create a bucket to store sensitive data, as shown in **Figure 3**.

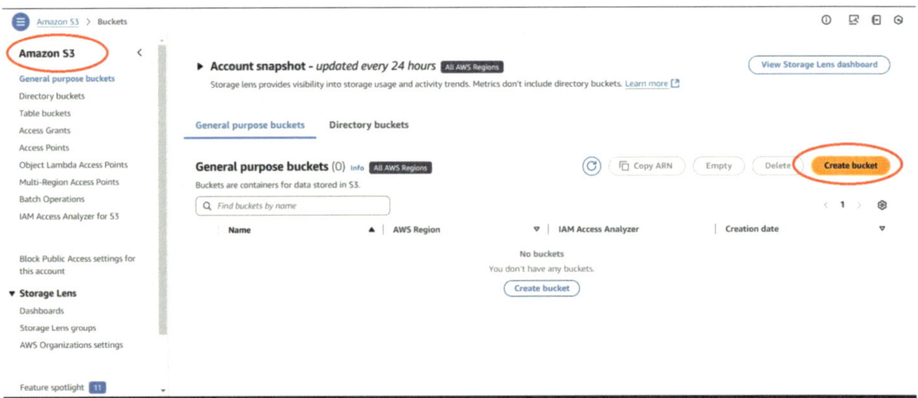

Figure 3.
Creation of S3 bucket.

5.1.4 Step 4

The bucket creation configuration entailed enabling public access to the bucket to allow Amazon Macie to detect the vulnerability of lack of privacy to stored objects via public access, as shown in **Figure 4**.

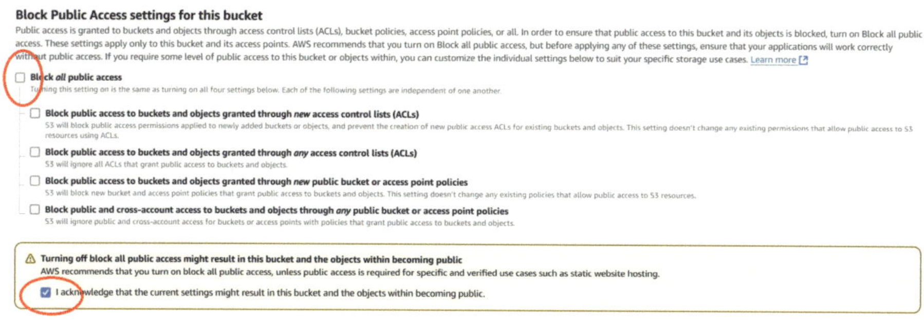

Figure 4.
Enable public access to the bucket.

5.1.5 Step 5

The "Server-side encryption with Amazon S3 Managed keys (SSE-S3)" option was selected as the encryption type in the Encryption configuration section, as shown in **Figure 5**. Bucket Key was enabled. Enabling the bucket key option via the dashboard minimizes the incurred encryption costs via lowered calls to the KMS.

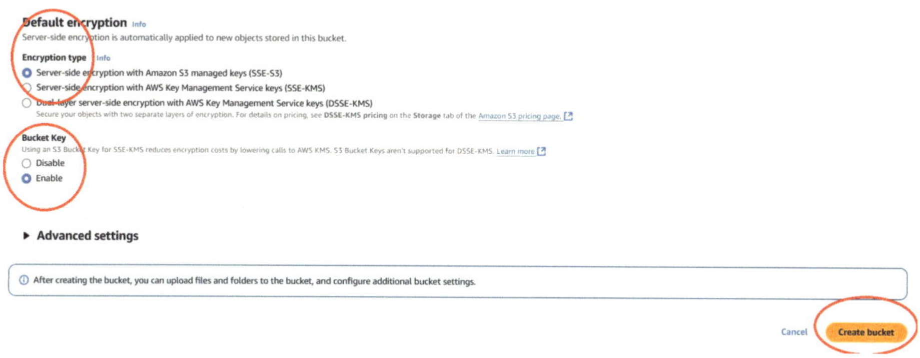

Figure 5.
SSE-S3 encryption type.

5.1.6 Step 6

The created bucket was selected, as shown in **Figure 6**. During bucket configuration, a unique bucket name was selected. Bucket names must be unique across all AWS accounts in all the AWS Regions within a partition.

5.1.7 Step 7

After creating the bucket, a document file was uploaded via the Amazon S3 dashboard, as shown in **Figure 7**. The document contained login credentials, which are sensitive information.

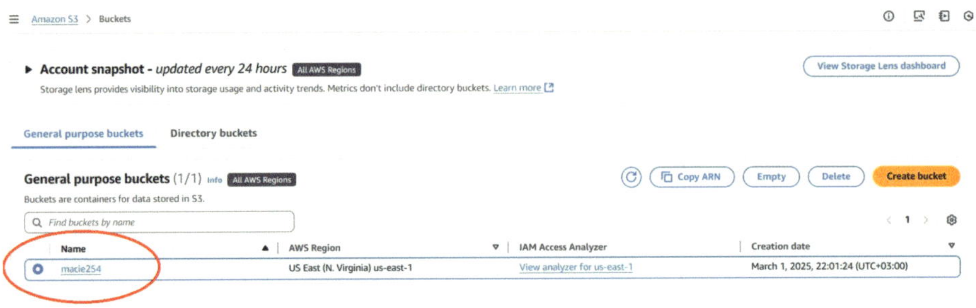

Figure 6.
Bucket selection.

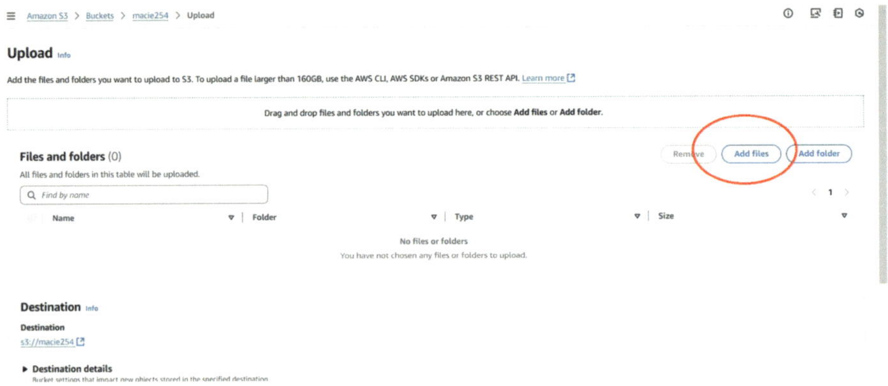

Figure 7.
File upload.

5.1.8 Step 8

After creating a user with the required permissions, the next step is to enable Amazon Macie for the AWS account. As shown in **Figure 8**, the Amazon Macie page enabled Macie for the account.

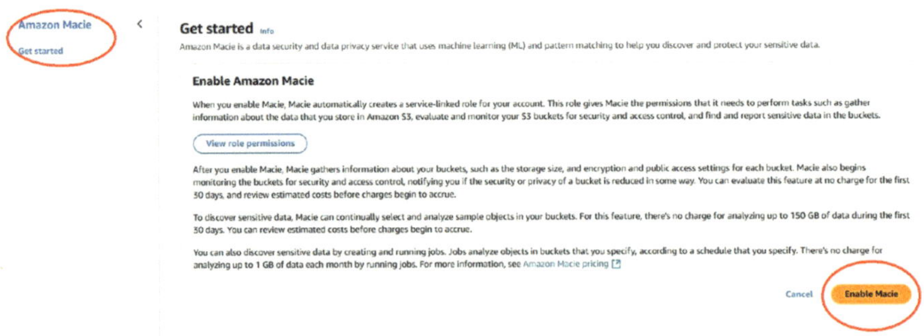

Figure 8.
Amazon Macie enabled.

5.1.9 Step 9

The Amazon Macie page enabled automated sensitive data discovery, as shown in **Figure 9**. When a user enables Macie, it automatically creates a service-linked role that allows it to call other AWS services and monitor AWS resources on its behalf.

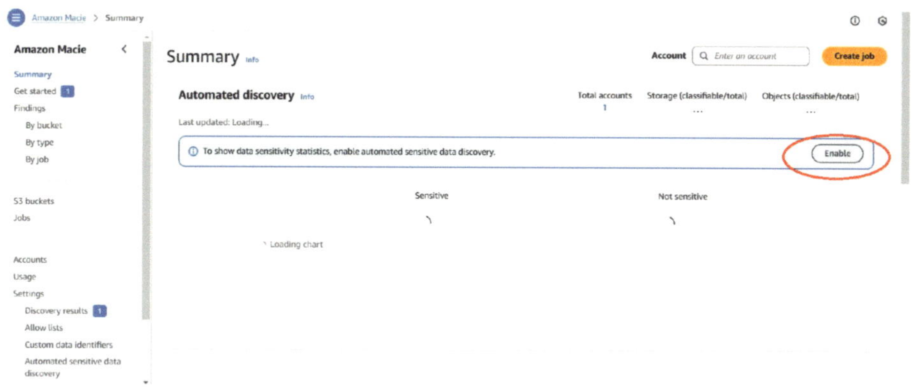

Figure 9.
Enable automated sensitive data discovery.

5.1.10 Step 10

Amazon Macie's findings page displayed policy findings, reporting potential issues as shown in **Figure 10**.

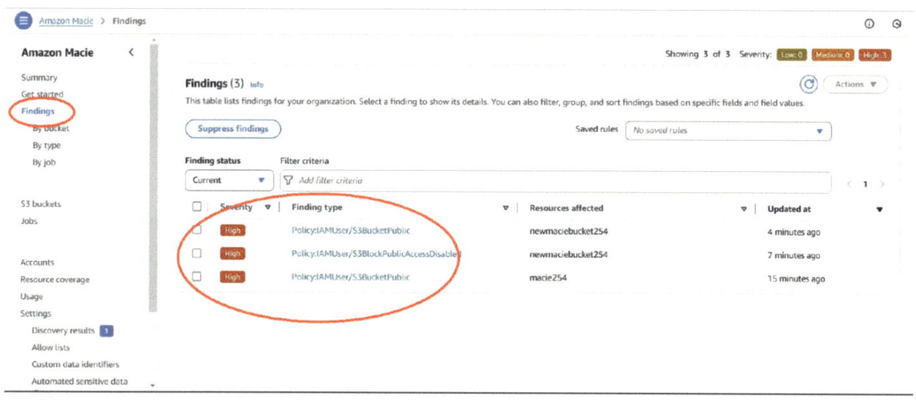

Figure 10.
Amazon Macie findings.

5.1.11 Step 11

The selection of a policy finding displayed details of the issue identified, which, in this case, grants public access to a bucket, as shown in **Figure 11**. Public access to a bucket introduces vulnerabilities via unauthorized access or cyber-attacks.

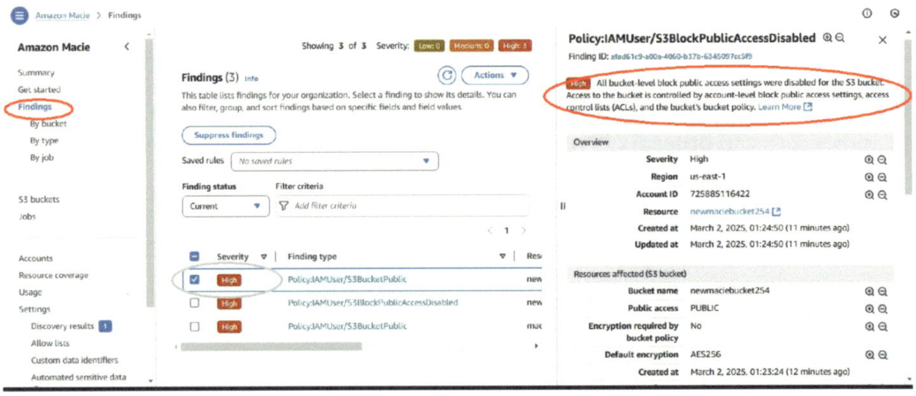

Figure 11.
Amacie's identification of a potential issue.

6. Results

The experiment was performed in the AWS cloud platform via Amazon Macie. Requirements for the experiments entailed the creation of an Amazon S3 bucket and the storage of text files with sensitive data consisting of AWS login credentials. The bucket configuration allowed public access, a vulnerability that exposed the stored sensitive information to unauthorized access or cyber-attacks. AWS IAM dashboard was used to create a user, and permissions were added via the attachment of "AmazonMacieFullAccess," an AWS-managed policy granting the user access to the Amazon Macie console and API operations. After permissions and bucket set up, the researcher enabled Amazon Macie, which automatically creates a service-linked role that allows monitoring of AWS resources on behalf of the user. Thereafter, Macie evaluated and monitored the created bucket for security and access control issues. The findings section in Mazon Macie's navigation pane helped view Macie's findings regarding automated sensitive data discovery for the created bucket. The findings revealed policy violations, particularly public access to the bucket, highlighting security and privacy issues.

The results relied on Hands-On, which was performed via the AWS account. AWS provides customers with Amazon Macie, which uses ML and pattern matching to provide insights into data security risks. Additionally, Macie enables automated protection against identified potential risks. Furthermore, Macie automates the discovery and reporting of sensitive data. The results demonstrated that Amazon Macie effectively reported potential issues with the security or privacy of cloud storage. Macie successfully reported sensitive data findings via automated sensitive data discovery. The results demonstrated Macie's capability to use ML to identify patterns and provide insights into data security risks via automation. Macie's data sampling techniques minimized the quantity of data scanned, reducing the costs of using the AI-driven cybersecurity framework. Macie's minimal computing resources to identify potential issues and provide action calls proved that the AI model relied on algorithms that helped reduce energy consumption, promoting sustainability.

Cloud technology that uses AI models allows users to scale the accessed cloud computing services quickly, helping avoid expenses of expensive idle resources or reduce problems due to insufficient capacity of the resources. Cloud computing also helps organizations increase speed and agility regarding access to computing resources such as AI-driven cybersecurity frameworks, which are a click away. Cloud computing also helps users deploy their AI-driven cybersecurity applications that respond to threats within minutes.

7. Conclusion

Cloud computing has revolutionized how modern organizations store, process, and manage data with scalability, flexibility, and cost efficiency. However, migration of computing resources to the cloud presents privacy and security risk challenges due to cyber threats, which are ever-evolving. Traditional security measures have become incapable of dealing with these ever-evolving threats, necessitating the integration of AI and ML into cloud security frameworks. AI-driven cybersecurity frameworks analyze vast datasets to help identify patterns ideal for anomaly detection and response to threats, enabling automation of defense mechanisms in cloud environments.

This chapter performed an experiment on the AWS cloud platform by using Amazon Macie as the AI-driven cybersecurity framework. Amazon Macie is an AWS security tool that uses ML to analyze AMazon S3 buckets and identify threats. Macie uses policy findings to report identified issues. Amazon S3 buckets were configured to allow public access, a practice that AWS highly discourages. Enabling public access to storage buckets introduces vulnerabilities as all users, including cybercriminals, have access to the stored data. The simulation showed Amazon Macie identifying the vulnerability of allowing public access via policy findings that were generated within minutes. The automation of Amazon Macie threat detection helped reduce computational operations that consume energy, promoting sustainability.

Amazon Macie's automated sensitivity jobs operations were in compliance with relevant regulations. Amazon Macie's operations were ethical as the AI model allowed users to review the policy findings and make necessary adjustments accordingly. The complexity issue normally associated with traditional security measures was addressed by Amazon Macie's simplicity of usage via automated operations. Furthermore, the AI model can scale to optimize computing resource usage, enabling sustainability.

Author details

Waleed Almuseelem
Faculty of Computing and Information Technology (FCIT), University of Tabuk, Tabuk, Saudi Arabia

*Address all correspondence to: waleedalmuseelem@ut.edu.sa

References

[1] Mamidi SR. The role of AI and machine learning in enhancing cloud security. Journal of Artificial Intelligence General Science (JAIGS). 2024;**3**(1):403-417

[2] Olabanji SO, Marquis Y, Adigwe CS, Ajayi SA, Oladoyinbo TO, Olaniyi OO. AI-driven cloud security: Examining the impact of user behavior analysis on threat detection. Asian Journal of Research in Computer Science. 2024;**17**(3):57-74

[3] Oduri S. Integrating AI into cloud security: Future trends and technologies. Webology. 2019;**16**:386-395

[4] Harris, Lorenzaj. Sustainable Cloud Computing: AI-Driven Solutions for Resource Efficiency. 2024. Available from: https://www.researchgate.net/publication/385287060_Sustainable_Cloud_Computing_AI-Driven_Solutions_for_Resource_Efficiency

[5] Nama P. Integrating AI with cloud computing: A framework for scalable and intelligent data processing in distributed environments. International Journal of Science and Research Archive. 2022;**06**(02):280-291

[6] Muppa KR. Advancing cloud security with AI-enhanced AWS identity and access management. International Research Journal of Engineering & Applied Sciences, IRJEAS. 2022;**10**(1):25-28

[7] Abdullahi M, Baashar Y, Alhussian H, Alwadain A, Aziz N, Capretz LF, et al. Detecting cybersecurity attacks in the internet of things using artificial intelligence methods: A systematic literature review. Electronics. 2022;**11**(2):198

[8] Aldridge I, Martin P. ESG in Corporate Filings: An AI Perspective. 17 November 2022. Available from: https://ssrn.com/abstract=4279479 or http://dx.doi.org/10.2139/ssrn.4279479

[9] Aruna ER, Reddy ARM, Sunitha KVN. Secure SDLC using security patterns 2.0. In: IOT with Smart Systems: Proceedings of ICTIS 2021, Volume 2. Singapore: Springer; 2022. pp. 699-708

[10] Gundu SR, Charanarur P, Chandelkar KK, Samanta D, Poonia RC, Chakraborty P. Sixth-generation (6G) Mobile cloud security and privacy risks for AI system using high-performance computing implementation. Wireless Communications and Mobile Computing. 2022;(1):4397610

[11] Ismatullaev UVU, Kim S-H. Review of the factors affecting acceptance of AI-infused systems. Human Factors. 2024;**66**(1):126-144

[12] Sudheer A. The Integration of AI in Cloud Security and Compliance: Key Opportunities and Challenges. 2024. Available from: https://www.infosys.com/services/microsoft-cloud-business/documents/integration-ai.pdf

[13] AWS. What is Amazon Macie? 2025. Available from: https://docs.aws.amazon.com/macie/latest/user/what-is-macie.html